SEVEN
WORDS

SEVEN WORDS

HOW THE SEVEN LETTERS OF
REVELATION SPEAK TO US TODAY

JOSHUA BROOKS

XULON PRESS

Xulon Press
2301 Lucien Way #415
Maitland, FL 32751
407.339.4217
www.xulonpress.com

xulon PRESS

© 2019 by Joshua Brooks

All rights reserved solely by the author. The author guarantees all contents are original and do not infringe upon the legal rights of any other person or work. No part of this book may be reproduced in any form without the permission of the author. The views expressed in this book are not necessarily those of the publisher.

Unless otherwise indicated, Scripture quotations taken from the Holy Bible, New International Version (NIV). Copyright © 1973, 1978, 1984, 2011 by Biblica, Inc.™. Used by permission. All rights reserved.

Printed in the United States of America.

ISBN-13: 978-1-54566-319-6

To my bride, Amanda.
I'm so thankful I get to serve Jesus and His Bride with you.
I love you, infinity for eternity.

CONTENTS

1. Revelation: It's All About Jesus 1
2. Jesus' Word to the Church at Ephesus:
   LOVE 17
3. Jesus' Word to the Church at Smyrna:
   COURAGE 43
4. Jesus' Word to the Church at Pergamum:
   PURITY 65
5. Jesus' Word to the Church at Thyatira:
   REPENTANCE...87
6. Jesus' Word to the Church at Sardis:
   REMEMBER..115
7. Jesus' Word to the Church at Philadelphia:
   PERSEVERANCE....................................... 139
8. Jesus' Word to the Church at Laodicea:
   HUMILITY.. 159
9. Jesus in Me > Me Trying Harder....................177
Endnotes 183

1
REVELATION: IT'S ALL ABOUT JESUS

I USED TO AVOID THE BOOK OF REVELATION like the plague. It's not exactly an easy read. So-called prophecy experts have only added to the confusion with their bizarre speculations and prognostications. History is riddled with such examples. Like the self-proclaimed end-times scholar who predicted Jesus would return in 1988. He even wrote a book: *88 Reasons Why the Rapture Will Be in 1988.*[1] It sold over three million copies.

I remember, as a freshman in high school, overhearing Christian classmates talk about how doing homework was a waste of time. Jesus would be coming back before the end of the year. Evidently, the date of His return was spelled out in the Book of Revelation, if you knew how to interpret it. I had a moment of panic as I contemplated what that might mean for me, since I wasn't following Jesus at the time. But when January 1, 1989 came along, and Jesus still hadn't returned, I smugly dismissed the faith of my classmates and this so-called end-times expert.

Surprisingly, though, this prophecy guru refused to acknowledge defeat. Early that next year, he "revised his calculations," and wrote another book, declaring the 89 Reasons why Jesus would come back in 1989.[2] Sadly, thousands of people bought that book, too. G.K. Chesterton was right when he said, "Though Saint John saw many strange monsters in his vision, he saw no creature so wild as one of his own commentators."[3]

It's no wonder so many Christians avoid the Book of Revelation. Those claiming to be experts in interpreting it often end up looking like fools. Why should we think we'd fare any better? Perhaps it's best to study the other 65 books of the Bible, and leave this one alone. However, if we take that approach, we will miss out on part of God's *revelation*. In particular, we'll miss out on more of God's revelation *of Jesus*. After all, that's the title of the book: 'The Revelation *of Jesus Christ*' (Revelation 1:1). Darrell Johnson explains the significance of Revelation's title:

> Literally, the title is 'The Apocalypse of Jesus Christ.' Sadly in our time the word 'apocalypse' has come to mean, 'Oh no! Something terrible is about to happen!' Thus we sadly speak of storms and natural disasters as being 'of apocalyptic proportion.' I say 'sadly' because that is not at all what first-century people would have thought when they heard the word 'apocalypse.' They would have thought of something more inviting, something immediately impacting the way they lived 24/7. The word simply meant 'unveiling.' It was used of lifting a cover off a box or pulling back a curtain in the theatre. The word meant 'opening up.' Or more dynamically 'breaking through.' 'The Revelation *of Jesus Christ*' – keep this description clear in our minds and we will not go astray. The title is 'The Lifting of the Cover, The Pulling Back of the Curtain, The Opening Up, The Breaking Through of Jesus Christ…'; The book is all about Jesus Christ.[4]

The seven letters of Revelation 2 & 3, in particular, are all about Jesus. They are the very words of Jesus. I think that's why I hear Jesus speaking into my life so clearly when I read them. Sure, they were written to people in another part of the world (Asia Minor) a long time ago (A.D. 96). But the more I study these seven letters to these seven ancient churches, the more I realize how similar I am to the Christians who first received them. The words *they* needed to hear are the words *I* need to hear, too:

- Like the church at Ephesus, I can reduce Christianity to simply believing the right things and doing the right things. Right doctrine and strong morals are good, but they're not enough. Jesus wants to transform my heart so that I love Him and love people. That's why Jesus' word to the church at Ephesus is also His word to me: **LOVE.**
- Like the church at Smyrna, I can slip into fear: the fear of death, the fear of pain, the fear of the future, the fear of the unknown. Yes, bad things are going to happen in this fallen world. But Jesus doesn't want me to be paralyzed by fear. He wants to transform me into a courageous Christ-follower, willing to risk anything for Him. That's why Jesus' word to the church at Smyrna is also His word to me: **COURAGE.**
- Like the church at Pergamum, I can start making "little" moral compromises with the world, especially when I'm going through a difficult season of life. Not that I would outright deny Jesus. But I might give into temptation a little bit here and there – to distract myself from the pain, boredom or loneliness I'm feeling. Jesus, though, doesn't want me to compromise, even in seemingly small ways. That's why, in those moments of temptation, Jesus' word to the church at Pergamum is also His word to me: **PURITY.**
- Like the church at Thyatira, I can be blinded by the spirit of Jezebel, who seeks to seduce me into believing the lie that I can have Jesus AND whatever else my heart is craving. That's why, in those moments when my heart is chasing after something other than God, Jesus' word to the church at Thyatira is also His word to me: **REPENT.**
- Like the church at Sardis, I can forget what Jesus has done for me. Spiritual amnesia sets in, and pretty soon,

I'm living on auto-pilot, no longer awed by the gospel, or passionate about the things of His Kingdom. I'm just going through the motions. That's why Jesus' word to the church at Sardis is also His word to me: **REMEMBER**.
- Like the church at Philadelphia, I can get discouraged by all of the pain in this world and in my life. Waiting for 'happily ever after' can feel like a pipe dream. But the truth is: that day is coming. Jesus will return and establish His glorious Kingdom. That's why Jesus' word to the church at Philadelphia is also His word to me: **PERSEVERE**.
- Like the church at Laodicea, I can start to think that I can manage my life without Jesus' help; that I'm smart enough or resourceful enough to create a happy, meaningful life on my own. But that's a lie. I'll never get to a place where I don't need Jesus. That's why, when I slip into self-sufficiency, Jesus' word to the church at Laodicea is also His word to me: **HUMILITY**.

Jesus sent these letters to specific people in specific churches at a specific time in history. But these letters weren't written just for them. They were also written for us. In apocalyptic literature, "7" is the number of completeness. 7 churches, then, is the symbolic way of talking about the *whole* church. 7 letters is Jesus' way of addressing *every* church and *every* Christian. As Darrell Johnson says, "It turns out that the seven churches of Asia embody every major issue with which the church has struggled in every age in every cultural setting."[5]

No matter what's going on in my church (or in my life) – these seven letters have something to say to us today. If we're willing to take the time to understand what Jesus is saying in these letters, we'll hear Him speaking to us. We'll hear Him encouraging us where we've become discouraged, inspiring us where we've grown lethargic, reminding us of things we've forgotten, instructing us where we need wisdom, and correcting us where we've strayed. Jesus says if we have "ears to hear" what the Spirit is saying in these letters (2:7, 11, 17, 29; 3:6, 13, 22), we'll hear

Him speaking straight to our hearts, telling us exactly what we need to hear.

And that is my two-fold prayer for this book:

1) That you would understand what Jesus' words _meant_ for these first century churches (HISTORICAL MEANING)
2) So that you can apply what Jesus' words _mean_ for your life (PERSONAL APPLICATION)

Many commentaries are scholarly-focused, addressing the historical context and original meaning of the Scriptures, but not really connecting it to where we are living today. On the other hand, preachers typically jump to: "Here's what this Scripture *means* for your life," without doing the hard work of explaining what the text originally *meant*. Both are essential. My goal is to bridge the gap between the historical meaning of these letters and how their message can be applied to our lives today.

Historical Context of the Seven Letters

One of the most important contextual points of these letters is that they were not written from the safety and comfort of some plush, ivory tower. They were penned in exile, amidst persecution. When John, Jesus' scribe, introduces himself, he writes:

> "I, John, your brother and companion in the suffering and kingdom and patient endurance that are ours in Jesus, was on the island of Patmos because of the word of God and the testimony of Jesus."
> ~ Revelation 1:9

The Book of Revelation was written on Patmos, an island used by the Roman Empire as a prison for criminals and political traitors. John, nearly ninety years old by A.D. 96, was sent there for treason. Why? John says, "because of the word of God and the testimony of Jesus." John wouldn't stop telling people about Christ, so Rome tried to silence him up by banishing him.

Antagonism against Christianity had been growing throughout the first century. Tradition has it that Emperor Nero had the Apostle Paul beheaded and the Apostle Peter crucified upside down. Persecution got even worse under the reign of Emperor Domitian (A.D. 81-96), an insecure leader, who was constantly paranoid that someone was trying to overthrow him. Domitian's narcissism eventually led him to demand that everyone living in the empire worship him as "Lord and God." The litmus test for each one's loyalty was to confess, 'Caesar is Lord.' If they did, they lived. If they didn't, they were killed.

For most of the people living in the Roman Empire, confessing, 'Caesar is Lord' was not a big deal. But it was a big deal for followers of Jesus, which is why John refused to bow down to Caesar. The Empire could have killed him. That's what they did to thousands of other Christians. But they took another approach with John, perhaps because of his age. Some scholars say that Rome didn't want to make an old man a martyr, because his death might inspire other Christians to be more vocal about their faith in Jesus. And so, instead of killing John, they exiled him to Patmos, separating him from the churches he knew and loved. 6

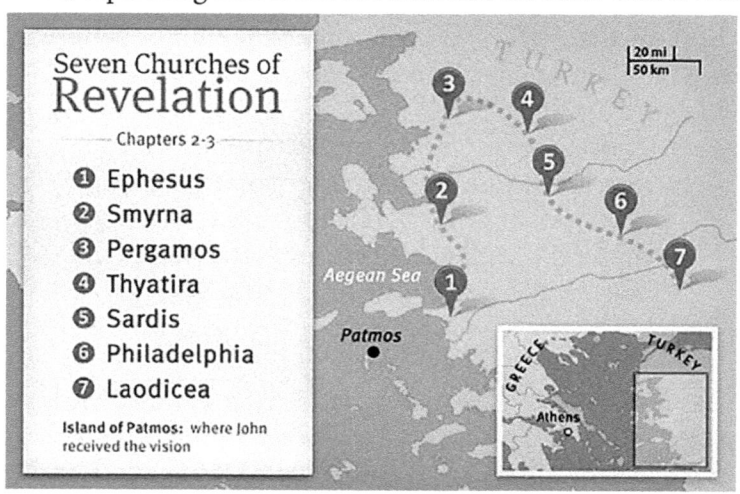

Seven Churches of Revelation
— Chapters 2-3 —

1. Ephesus
2. Smyrna
3. Pergamos
4. Thyatira
5. Sardis
6. Philadelphia
7. Laodicea

Island of Patmos: where John received the vision

All John could do on that remote island in the middle of the Mediterranean Sea was pray – which is what he was doing one Sunday when Jesus showed up:

> "On the Lord's Day I was in the Spirit, and I heard behind me a loud voice like a trumpet, which said, 'Write on a scroll what you see and send it to the seven churches: to Ephesus, Smyrna, Pergamum, Thyatira, Sardis, Philadelphia and Laodicea.'"
> ~ Revelation 1:10

Jesus wanted to give John and the seven churches something to encourage them. It probably wasn't what they expected, but it was exactly what they needed. Darrell Johnson writes:

> How does the Lord respond? By telling John to have the elders form 'A Task Force on Political Terror?' No. By giving John a set of new programs to be implemented in the various congregations on the mainland? No. By calling John to form a resistance movement? No. By giving John a strategy by which Christians could slowly displace pagans in public office? Not a bad thing to do, but no. By giving John more cash for the church's budget? No. How does Jesus respond? He lifts the cover; he pulls back the curtain. Jesus responds with a revelation; with an apocalypse; with an unveiling… with a powerful vision of who Jesus is.[7]

A powerful vision of who Jesus is.

That's what John needed more than anything else. That's what these seven churches needed more than anything else. That's what you and I need more than anything else: *a powerful vision of who Jesus is.*

Introducing Jesus

The first glimpse of Jesus comes in John's introduction:

> "To Him who loves us and has freed us from our sins by His blood, and has made us to be a kingdom and priests to serve his God and Father – to Him be glory and power for ever and ever! Amen."
> ~ Revelation 1:5-6

John doesn't even finish his introduction to the Book of Revelation without breaking into a doxology of praise to Jesus: "To Him be glory and power forever and ever!" (Rev 1:6). That will be our response, too, when our eyes are opened to Jesus and how much He loves us, which is the first of three transformational truths that John proclaims in these introductory verses.

1) Jesus loves us: "To Him who loves us..." (v5a)

Much of Revelation is confusing. Even the seven letters, which are easier to understand than the rest of the book, still require digging into the historical context of the first century to fully grasp what they're saying. But as confusing as Revelation might be in some places, there's nothing complicated about this verse: Jesus loves us.

I almost entitled this book, *Love Letters from Jesus*. Not because these seven letters are particularly sentimental, but because what Jesus says in them is absolutely motivated by His love for us. Even when He has challenging things to say to us in these letters, He says them because of how much He cares about us. Keep that in mind when Jesus is correcting, rebuking or warning us. He's doing it out of love – the way a good Father loves His children enough to discipline them, so they can grow up into maturity.

Revelation begins with a simple truth, one for which we don't have to be a scholar to figure out its meaning: *Jesus loves us*.

This reminds me of a story about a scholar, Dr. Karl Barth, arguably one of the most influential theologians of the twentieth century. His twelve-volume, *Church Dogmatics,* consists of over ten thousand pages of systematic theology, some of which (like Revelation) is not easy to comprehend. Despite the depth of his theology, though, there was also a very simple message at its core: *Christ's love for us.* This is best illustrated by something that happened toward the end of his life. Barth was touring the United States, speaking at several of our nation's top universities. And during a question and answer time following one of his lectures, a student asked: "Dr. Barth, you have written extensively on every aspect of theology and church history. I'm wondering if you could sum it up in a short sentence or two."

The room fell silent. Dr. Barth stood just there for a moment, carefully considering how to respond. Some of the professors and students who were there began to feel awkward that such a trifling question would be asked of such a brilliant scholar. Finally, Barth turned toward the student and succinctly replied, *"Jesus loves me, this I know, for the Bible tells me so."*

Like Karl Barth's writings, the Book of Revelation is complex, and in places, even downright confusing. But when you boil it down, one of the core truths of Revelation is that *Jesus loves us.*

2) Jesus died for our sins: "…and has freed us from our sins by His blood…" (v5b)

John doesn't just tell us *that* Jesus loves us. He follows up that truth by clarifying the *extent* of His love: that Jesus was willing to die for us to set us free from our sins. John is only five verses into the Book of Revelation, and he's already proclaiming the gospel, the good news of what God did for us in Christ at the cross!

I love this about John. Even into his nineties, even after leading the church for sixty years, even after countless sermons and retellings of stories about Jesus, even after writing the Fourth Gospel and multiple letters to multiple churches, John still can't help but lead off the Book of Revelation with a declaration of the gospel: *what Jesus did for us at the cross.*

This is a lesson for all of us, especially for those who have been Christians for a long time. Many believers have this idea that the gospel is like the diving board into the pool of Christianity. We know we need the gospel initially, to become a Christian. But after we jump in, we think we need to swim to "deeper" waters (beyond the gospel) to learn how to live as a Christian. The more I read the Bible, though, the more I see the gospel on every single page, in every single command, as both the motivation and the power for how we are to live. For example:

- When 1 Peter calls us to be faithful in the midst of suffering, that command is grounded in the gospel. Peter doesn't simply tell us to suck it up and persevere. He reminds us that Christ was willing to suffer for us, even dying on a cross (1 Pet 3:18). Therefore, based on the gospel, he calls us to be faithful in the midst of our suffering, too.
- When 2 Corinthians calls us to be generous, that command is grounded in the gospel. Paul doesn't just call us to stop being scrooges. He reminds us that Christ was generous with us, leaving the riches of Heaven and becoming poor – so that we might become rich (2 Cor 8:9). Therefore, based on the gospel, he calls us to be generous, too.
- When Ephesians calls husbands to love their wives, that command is grounded in the gospel. Paul doesn't threaten to call the Focus on the Family police if husbands don't love their wives. He reminds them that Christ so loved His Bride (the Church) that He died for her (Eph 5:25). Therefore, based on the gospel, he calls husbands to love their brides, too.

This is the pattern throughout the entire New Testament, including the seven letters of Revelation. These letters contain many commands to do certain things, and to stop doing other things. But John, in the introduction, grounds every one of these commands in the gospel, in the good news of what God did for us in Christ at the cross. As David Prior says, "We never move on from the cross of Christ, only into a more profound understanding of the cross."[8]

That's why John begins with the cross. If we don't understand what Jesus did for us there, we won't read the seven letters the way they're intended to be read. We'll read them as a to-do list, where we try to justify ourselves before God with our good behavior. We'll read them as a morality manual for how to live so that God will love us. We'll read them as a call to clean ourselves up so that God will accept us. But this is not how Jesus wants us to read these letters. He wants us to read these letters through the lens of how we're *already* justified, loved, and accepted – because of what He did for us at the cross – so that we're motivated to obey Him out of gratitude and joy, not out of guilt and fear.

So have you received the justification, love, and acceptance that Christ achieved for you at the cross? If not, then before you start reading these seven letters, and try to do all the things He's calling *you* to *do*, look first at what *He's* already *done* for you... and receive it.

3) Jesus has a purpose for our lives: "... made us to be a kingdom and priests to serve...." (v6)

The forgiveness of our sins isn't the only thing Jesus died for. His death wasn't just about getting us right with God, so we could go to Heaven when we die – as great as that will be. Jesus has a purpose for our lives *right now*. Jesus saves us so that we might become all that He created us to be: *a Kingdom of priests, who serve Him, and represent Him to the world*. After all, that's what "priests" do: they represent God to people, and point people to God. And that's what Jesus died for: that His people, having now been made right with God and filled with His Spirit – would become His image bearers, His priests, His ambassadors – bearing witness to the world of the good news of a King whose Kingdom is coming!

This has always been God's purpose – with Adam and Eve, with Israel, and now in Jesus:

- Adam and Eve were called to be His image bearers to all of creation (Gen 1:26-28)
- Israel was called to be a kingdom of priests to all of the other nations (Ex 19:5-6)
- Jesus' disciples are now called to take the gospel to the whole world (Matt 28:18-20)

Jesus saves us to become His priests to the world. Not in the sense that we wear priestly collars, or that we all become pastors, but that we all recognize the call on our lives to represent Jesus to the people around us, living our lives in a way that points to Him.

It's a tragedy when the gospel gets reduced to simply saying a prayer so we can go to Heaven (instead of Hell) when we die. If the gospel is only about going to Heaven when we die, then Christianity is just a religion for death, an eternal insurance policy to have in our back pocket that doesn't impact the way we live now. But that's not all Jesus is reaching for. Jesus wants us to become His ambassadors, taking the good news of His love and Lordship to the ends of the earth, participating in His epic story of redeeming and transforming people from every tribe, tongue, and nation (Rev 7:9). If we miss this, we miss the purpose for which Jesus died.

Salvation is not just about what God saves us *from*; it's about what God saves us *for*.

What does that mean for you and your life? It means that no matter your past, God wants to use you. It doesn't matter how messed up or flawed your life has been (or is), or how few gifts or talents you think you have to offer. When you put your trust in Christ, you are not only saved *from* sin, death, and Hell; you are saved *for* a purpose of eternal significance. God is inviting you to join Him in the greatest rescue mission the world has ever known.

And that is where the seven letters come into play. Since Jesus has such a grand purpose for our lives, there are things He wants to say to us so we become the people He created us to be, living out the purpose for which He saved us. That's the heart behind these seven letters.

Jesus loves us.
Jesus died for our sins.
Jesus has a purpose for our lives.

In Preparation for the Seven Letters

Before you try to take in and take on all that Jesus wants to say to you in these seven letters, you need to first appropriate who He is and what He's done for you. Have you?

1) Do you really believe Jesus loves *you*?

Not just that He loves you because He's doctrinally obligated to love everybody, but that He really, truly, loves *you*.

2) Do you really believe Jesus died for *you* so that *your* sins could be forgiven?

As a pastor, I've talked with so many people (even people who have grown up in the church), who secretly wonder, "Can *my* sins really be forgiven? *All* of them? Even the ones I'm too ashamed to talk about?" The good news of the gospel is that Jesus paid the price for *all* of your sins. Not just some of them. Every one of them. And you can receive that forgiveness right now – not by promising to be the perfect Christian between now and when you die. Newsflash: you'll fall short. No, you can receive forgiveness by confessing your sins, putting your faith in what Jesus did for you at the cross, and entrusting the leadership of your life to Him. You don't have to live another day wondering about whether or not your sins can really be forgiven. You can receive His forgiveness right now, in this very moment.

3) Do you really believe Jesus has a purpose for *your* life?

For many Christians, their relationship with God is simply an arrangement to go to Heaven (instead of Hell) when they die. But Jesus went to the cross for so much more than that. Jesus went to the cross so we might be forgiven, made right with God, and be filled with His Spirit, SO THAT we could become His image bearers, His priests, His Kingdom ambassadors – to the rest of the world. Are you ready to step into His purpose for your life?

My Prayer for You

My prayer, as you begin this study, is that you would be able to hear the Spirit of Christ say to you: "I love you. I went to the cross for you, so your sins could be forgiven, and so you could step into the glorious purpose for which I saved you."

Once you hear Jesus speaking these truths to your heart (and you receive them personally), you'll *want* to listen to what He has to say to you in these letters. You'll come to these letters with a spirit of anticipation, *longing* for Him to speak to you, to shape you, to inspire you, to correct you, and to equip to live out His purpose for your life.

So before jumping into the seven letters, take a few minutes right now to ask Jesus to open up your heart to these truths – so that you can hear them and receive them personally.

Digging Deeper

1) Do an internet search for *Falling Plates*, and then watch this powerful 4-minute video, which illustrates the gospel.

2) Listen to the gospel-centered song, *Man of Sorrows*. Put it on your playlist during your study of the seven letters, as an audible reminder that "we don't move on from the cross of Christ, only into a more profound understanding of the cross."

3) Jesus has a purpose for your life now. But that means surrendering to His chisel. Get on the internet and watch the 5-minute video, *God's Chisel*, as a way of preparing yourself for the shaping work Jesus will do on you through the seven letters.

2

JESUS' WORD TO THE CHURCH AT EPHESUS: LOVE

WITH TODAY'S TECHNOLOGY, I CAN SEE just about any church building on the planet. But technology has its limitations. I can see the *outside* of the church building, but I can't see into the *hearts* of the people who are inside the church. There's no app for that!

But there is One who *can* see into the hearts of people. According to Revelation 1:14, Jesus has piercing eyes, like "blazing fire." The opening words of the letter to the church at Ephesus tell us Jesus sees everything we're doing. He knows everything about us. He's aware of every detail of our lives. How? Because, even though we don't see Him, He is walking among us:

> "To the angel of the church in Ephesus write: These are the words of him who holds the seven stars in his right hand and walks among the seven golden lampstands."
> ~ Revelation 2:1

What are the "seven golden lampstands?"

Revelation 1:20 tells us: "the seven lampstands *are* the seven churches."

This is Revelation's way of saying Jesus is walking among *all of His churches* (remember "7" = complete). In other words, Jesus is walking among all His churches, perfectly aware of all that's happening in the lives of His people. That's why, at the beginning of each letter to each church, Jesus says, "I know…"

- Ephesus: "I know your deeds" (Rev 2:1)
- Smyrna: "I know your afflictions" (Rev 2:8)
- Pergamum: "I know where you live" (Rev 2:13)
- Thyatira: "I know your deeds" (Rev 2:18)
- Sardis: "I know your deeds" (Rev 3:1)
- Philadelphia: "I know your deeds" (Rev 3:8)
- Laodicea: "I know your deeds" (Rev 3:15)

Jesus knows everything about us. He knows where we're being faithful, and where we're trapped in habits and patterns of sin. He knows where we're experiencing victory, and where we need encouragement. He knows where we're walking in obedience, and where we've strayed and need correction. He is with us. He knows us. He knows us so well that He tells us exactly what we need to hear, which is what He does in these seven letters, beginning with the letter to the church at Ephesus.

Why is Ephesus First?

Seven letters to seven cities meant seven stops for the mail carrier sailing from Patmos. Ephesus was the first stop on the journey. It was one of the most significant cities in the entire Roman Empire, a cosmopolitan urban center characterized by wealth and political power.

Ephesus was most famous for being the worship center of Artemis, the goddess of hunting and childbirth (talk about a unique gift mix)! According to legend, the image of Artemis fell from the sky to grace their city (Acts 19:35). The people of Ephesus were proud of Artemis being their goddess. She was their claim to fame. She put them on the map. She drew people to their city from all over the Empire. She was the reason for their bustling economy. And so, in response to all that Artemis had done for them, Ephesus' devotion to her was absolute. They even built a temple in her honor, twice the size of a football field.

Allegiance to Artemis was so strong that anyone who said or did anything to question her authority opened themselves up to persecution. That's why Paul's missionary efforts in Ephesus were met with such opposition (Acts 19). The gospel called into question the claim that Artemis was a goddess. That then impacted their local economy, since fewer Artemis statues were being purchased. As a result, it wasn't long before a riot broke out, with the staunchest Artemis worshipers and vendors threatening to kill Paul and his companions.

Despite such hostility, though, the gospel took root in hearts, and a church was planted in Ephesus. Not only were souls saved, but lives were transformed and remade into the image of the true God, whose grace really had fallen from Heaven upon their city. The church at Ephesus became a beacon of truth and integrity in a city full of idolatry.

And yet that didn't mean they were a perfect church. There was much in them worthy of commendation, but Jesus cared enough about them to call out what was still lacking. As you'll see in this letter, Jesus both praises them for all they're doing well, and calls them out for neglecting the most important thing: LOVE.

> "To the angel of the church in Ephesus write:
>
> These are the words of him who holds the seven stars in his right hand and walks among the seven golden lampstands. I know your deeds, your hard work and your perseverance. I know that you cannot tolerate wicked people, that you have tested those who claim to be apostles but are not, and have found them false. You have persevered

and have endured hardships for my name, and have not grown weary.

Yet I hold this against you: You have forsaken the love you had at first. Consider how far you have fallen! Repent and do the things you did at first. If you do not repent, I will come to you and remove your lampstand from its place. But you have this in your favor: You hate the practices of the Nicolaitans, which I also hate.

Whoever has ears, let them hear what the Spirit says to the churches. To the one who is victorious, I will give the right to eat from the tree of life, which is in the paradise of God."

~ Revelation 2:1-7

In Praise of the Church at Ephesus

There's quite a bit that Jesus affirms in the Ephesian believers:

- They've worked hard
- They've persevered in the face of opposition
- They've confronted evil, "hating the practice of the Nicolaitans," a heretical sect that twisted God's grace into a license to sin
- They've fought for the truth, and not tolerated false teaching
- They've endured hardship for His name, and haven't grown weary

In a culture that was antagonistic toward Christianity, the believers in Ephesus stood strong, refusing to give into the idolatry or moral decay of the city. They were resolved to teach the truth and live faithfully for Christ, even in a hostile setting that

JESUS' WORD TO THE CHURCH AT EPHESUS: LOVE

viewed their claims as narrow-minded and bigoted. Not surprisingly, the church of Ephesus became the spiritual epicenter of early Christianity. Its commitment to the truth makes sense, too, when you look back on their history, and consider the caliber of teachers, pastors and apostles who taught them.

Historical Background

In A.D. 52, Priscilla and Aquila were the first Christian teachers on the ground in Ephesus. There wasn't even a formal church established there yet, but Priscilla and Aquila, co-ministers of the Apostle Paul, became the appointed teachers of the region. This couple was gifted in disciple-making and mentoring, and trained future church leaders like Apollos (Acts 18).

In A.D. 53-55, Paul went to Ephesus, and taught them for over two years, which was his longest stay in any one place. As a result of Paul's teaching and preaching ministry in Ephesus, the Book of Acts says: "The Word of the Lord spread widely and grew in power" (Acts 19:20).

In A.D. 56, just before Paul left Ephesus, he called a meeting with the church elders, to tell them some things the Spirit had prompted him to say. In his final words to them, Paul warned them to watch out for false teachers: "I know that after I leave, savage wolves will come in among you and will not spare the flock. Even from your own number men will arise and distort the truth in order to draw away disciples after them. So be on your guard!" (Acts 20:29-31).

The church at Ephesus never forgot Paul's warning, and stayed on guard against false teachers. Four decades later, they remained diligent in combatting false teachings of all kinds (Rev 2:2).

In A.D. 63, Paul commissioned Timothy, his apprentice and spiritual son, to lead the church at Ephesus. Paul appointed him to this post with a very specific assignment in mind. At the beginning of his letter, Paul tells him: "Stay there in Ephesus so that you may command certain men not to teach false doctrines any longer!" (1 Timothy 1:3).

That was Timothy's primary job as shepherd of this church: to guard the truth of the gospel against false teachers. And Timothy was faithful to that assignment. He pastored and taught the church at Ephesus for several years, until he was most likely executed (by Rome) for his faith.

Around A.D. 70-95, the Apostle John, the beloved disciple of Jesus and the author of five books of the New Testament, became the pastor at Ephesus. According to church history, John taught and shepherded the church at Ephesus for twenty plus years, until he was exiled to Patmos for his commitment to "the word of God and the testimony of Jesus" (Rev 1:10).

Think about the forty-year run of teachers at this church: Priscilla and Aquila, the Apostle Paul, Pastor Timothy, and the Apostle John. No local church in history has ever had the kind of roll call of teachers that Ephesus enjoyed for four decades. As a result, the church was laser focused on the importance of truth, heeding Paul's warnings (from A.D. 56), and ferreting out false teachers and bad doctrine. Jesus says so in his letter to them (Rev 2:2).

What was Missing?

Despite all that the church at Ephesus was doing well: guarding the truth, working hard for the Kingdom, and calling out sin – they were still missing something: *love*.

> "Yet I hold this against you: You have forsaken the love you had at first."
> ~ Revelation 2:4

The believers at Ephesus had so much going for them, except the one thing Jesus wanted most: love. Evidently, believing the right things and doing a lot of good stuff is not all that Jesus is looking for. As Darrell Johnson writes:

> This church is buzzing with doing. They have all kinds of ministries and programs going. Its

members are actively involved, all working for the advancement of the Kingdom… They're pushing themselves for the Kingdom. They're diligent and conscientious… They're faithfully standing strong against opposition. They're resisting the pressure to bow their knee to Caesar. They're refusing to participate in the idolatrous worship of Artemis… They're committed to purity of life and to teaching right doctrine…9

That sounds like a good church to me. In fact, if there was ever such a thing as a perfect church, Ephesus looked the part. They would have been the most likely host for the conference: *How to Be a Successful Church.* But that's not how Jesus viewed them. Despite all they were doing well, Jesus says: "Yet I hold this against you: you have forsaken the love you had at first."

To understand what Jesus is getting at here, it's important to know that (in the Greek) there is no object for the forsaken love. Jesus doesn't say, 'You've forsaken your love *for Me.*' Neither does He say, 'You've forsaken your love *for each other.*' He says, 'You've forsaken the love you had *at first.*' The emphasis is on the word, 'first,' which many scholars agree implies that the church had forsaken both their love for Jesus *and* their love for each other.

Part 1: Loving Jesus

Despite all the good things the Ephesian church was doing, their love for Jesus had grown cold. And evidently, this was a serious matter. Jesus told the Ephesians that if they didn't remedy their love problem, He would "remove their lampstand" (Rev 2:5). This is equivalent to saying: *they would no longer be part of His Church.* In other words, without a white-hot love for Jesus, we might as well close the doors of the church, cancel the services, and scrap the programs. It doesn't matter how accurate our teaching is, how moral our behavior is, or how diligent our service is. If there isn't a deep love for Jesus that marks us, we've missed the point.

Jesus is not interested in a group of people who gather in His name, who are just going through the motions of church. He wants a people who *love* Him, with the kind of affection and devotion a new bride has for her groom. That's why, throughout the Bible, the analogy used to describe God's relationship to His people is that of a Groom and a Bride.

Groom and Bride in the Bible

- In Exodus, God rescued Israel out of slavery to Egypt, and drew her into a covenant relationship with Himself.
- In Joshua, God provided her a beautiful home in the Promised Land, a land flowing with milk and honey.
- According to Judges, though, it wasn't long before Israel began to cheat on God with other lovers: worshiping the gods of her neighbors, pseudo-gods that promised comfort, fertility, and security. Soon, she was giving her heart (and everything else) to these gods.
- According to the Prophets, God didn't just tell Israel to stop sinning and start behaving. He was reaching for something deeper. He was reaching for her heart. So in Jeremiah, God pleaded with His wayward people, "Remember the devotion of your youth, how as a bride you loved me and followed me" (2:2). God longed for Israel to remember all that He had done for her, so that she might love Him again, like she did *at first*.

It's mind-boggling that the Creator of the universe would allow His heart to be so vulnerable to rejection and betrayal. But that's the picture of God we see in the Bible. Instead of responding to Israel's adultery by issuing her divorce papers, God continues to pursue her.

- According to the Gospels, God became even more vulnerable, putting on frail humanity, and entering our world – in pursuit of His wayward Bride. Still, we spurned Him, crying out, "Crucify Him!" Even this didn't keep God from loving us, though. At the cross, He demonstrated the depth of His love, dying for our sins, even while we rejected Him (Romans 5:8).
- According to the final book of the Bible, God's pursuit, rescue, and redemption of His Bride will culminate in what Revelation 19:9 calls "the marriage supper of the Lamb" – a fitting conclusion to what God has been after from the very beginning.

All of history is moving toward a *marriage* between Christ and His Bride, the Church. And a marriage should be marked by love. This is why a diminishing love for Jesus is such a problem. If it's just religion and ritual that Jesus is looking for, it doesn't really matter whether we love Him. But if we're His *Bride*, and our love for Him grows *cold*, that's not the kind of marriage Jesus is looking for – which is why He calls us to "love Him like we did at first" – like we loved Him when we first realized the depth of what He did for us.

That's the Ephesians' root problem: they don't love Jesus like they used to.

For many of us, that's our root problem, too. Every sin we're battling, our lack of passion to pray, our lack of desire to read His Word, our lack of urgency to share our faith with others, our lack of self-control – it all gets traced back to this: we don't love Jesus like we used to.

So, if that's our root problem, then what's the solution? Jesus tells us: "Remember the height from which you have fallen. Repent and do the things you did at first" (Rev 2:5). These are the two things we need to do if our love for Jesus has grown cold:

1) <u>Remember</u>. Think back to those days when our eyes were opened to what Jesus did for us.

2) <u>Repent</u>. Do those things we used to do when our love and gratitude for Jesus was strong.

In a sense, Jesus is calling us to renew our vows.

Renewing Our Vows

It's impossible for me to read Jesus' word to *His* bride – without thinking about my relationship to *my* bride. Amanda and I have been married for twenty-two years. I love her more today than the day we got married. Sadly, I don't always show it. I can slip into auto-pilot, going through the motions of marriage, taking for granted that she chose to spend the rest of her life with me.

While studying this letter, I was inspired to spend time reflecting on the honeymoon chapter our relationship. I thought about the things I used to do to show her love: writing her letters late into the night, surprising her with gifts, being creative in the planning of dates. And the thing is – it wasn't a chore to do those things. I *wanted* to do them.

If you're married, though, you know what can happen, if you're not intentional.

Amanda is amazing, but I still feel the gravitational pull toward taking her for granted. So one of the ways I guard myself against "forsaking the love I had for her at first" is by remembering and repenting: *reflecting back on how grateful I was that day when she chose to spend the rest of her life with me, and doing the things I used to do for her.*

I don't want to sound like I'm doing those things as much as I could be doing them. Nor do I want to send the message that doing these things comes as naturally now as it did during the honeymoon phase of our relationship. It requires more intentionality. But when I do the things I used to do for Amanda, there is often a renewing in me of that "first love" affection. In a sense, I'm transported back in time, and reminded of how grateful I was that day she married me – which then spurs me on to serve her all the more. This is why I often tell couples who are "falling out

JESUS' WORD TO THE CHURCH AT EPHESUS: LOVE

of love" to do those things they used to do for each other during the honeymoon chapter of their story. It's amazing how often it kick-starts affections that have grown cold.

The analogy breaks down, but I think this is what Jesus is reaching for when He calls us to remember and repent. He wants us to:

1) Remember how we loved Him when we first realized He chose *us* to spend eternity with Him
2) Do those things we did when we were living in that reality

This is what motivated me to do another exercise: reflecting back on the things I used to do when I was in the "honeymoon" phase of my relationship *with Jesus,* when my eyes were first opened to all He did to save me. I don't want to sound like a Pharisee, applauding myself for my devotion to Jesus. My intent is simply to be transparent about the kind of remembering and repenting Jesus is reaching for in this letter. So here are a few of the memories that came to my mind as I thought back to the honeymoon chapter of my relationship with Christ.

- I remember working the late shift at Denny's, and being so excited to get off work, because I wanted to get home and <u>read the Bible</u> into the early hours of the morning.
- I remember taking the bus into downtown Seattle, walking the streets, inviting homeless people to the Bread of Life soup kitchen, <u>serving</u> them a hot meal, sharing the gospel with them, and praying for them.
- I remember waking up early to <u>pray</u> for guys on my dorm floor to come to Christ.
- I remember how excited I was to go to church on Sunday mornings – even if I had stayed up late the night before. I couldn't imagine sleeping in and taking a pass on <u>worshiping the One who had died for me</u>.
- I remember approaching guys in my dorm and asking if they had anyone encouraging them in areas where they

were tempted. I didn't have an official ministry role, but I put together <u>accountability groups</u>, to help these guys grow spiritually.
- I remember finding ways to <u>share my faith</u> with anyone who would listen – whether it was with guys in my dorm, the homeless, or friends and family back home. I was always on the look-out for opportunities to tell people about Jesus.

After writing down these memories, I then took a closer look at the list, and began to underline the specific things I *did* – out of my love for Jesus:

- **Reading God's Word**
- **Serving the poor**
- **Praying for the lost**
- **Worshiping God even when I was tired**
- **Being in (and encouraging) accountability relationships**
- **Sharing my faith with those who didn't yet know Christ**

As I looked at my list, I realized these are probably the things Jesus would remind me of *today*, if He were to send *me* a letter and say: "Repent and do the things you did at first."

The reality is Jesus *did* send this letter to me. This letter isn't just for the church at Ephesus. It's for me, too, which means I *should* be doing these things today – in one form or another. The particulars might look a little different, because I'm married now, not single; I live in the suburbs now, not the city; I'm a pastor now, not a college student. But the heart of what I *did* I should still be *doing* in one form or another – even if I'm not feeling it in the same way as when I was in the honeymoon phase of my relationship with Jesus.

It's easy for lists to lead to legalism. But just because I do something that's on a list doesn't mean it's an insincere way to show Jesus my love. And just because I don't *feel* like doing it doesn't mean I shouldn't. Jesus is honored when we do the things

JESUS' WORD TO THE CHURCH AT EPHESUS: LOVE

He's calling us to do regardless of whether or not we're "feeling it." Our culture is feeding us the lie, that in order to be authentic, we must only do those things we feel like doing. But the Scriptures say if we only do what we feel like doing, we're "slaves to the flesh" (Romans 6). And Christ wants to set us free from the flesh – to live for Him!

Ideally, obedience to Jesus is fueled by our love for Him. That's why it's a good idea to stir up our affections for Jesus. And the primary way we do that is by reminding ourselves of who Jesus is and what He's done for us. If we try to love Jesus without first being gripped by the immensity of His love for us, then our efforts to obey Him will be a white-knuckle exercise in religious duty. Gritting our teeth and trying really hard to obey is not the way to go. A better path is to draw close to the cross and dwell on all that Jesus did for us. Then our obedience will shift from mere duty to a desire to obey Him out of love. I can testify to this personally.

It happened years ago. I had been a pastor for more than a decade. I was living my life in service to Jesus and the Church. But I had lost some of my sense of awe at what Jesus had done for me. I was still doing good stuff, like the believers at Ephesus. But it was mostly out of a sense of duty. Then during a prayer time on vacation, away from all of my ministry responsibilities, I sensed the Lord wooing me to draw near to the cross. At first, I didn't understand. I knew the theological significance of the cross. At least I thought I did. But looking back, I realize now what Jesus was doing. He was inviting me to gaze more deeply at what He had done for me, so He could recapture my heart and rekindle my love for Him.

Shortly after this experience in prayer, I providentially came upon *The Cross of Christ,* by John Stott. I don't know how to describe what happened next, except to say that God used this book to reawaken me to the riches of His sacrifice. I read it through three times. I pored over all of the Scriptures referenced in it that spoke of what Jesus was doing when He gave his life for me. At the risk of sounding sappy or sentimental, I found myself falling in love with Jesus again.

Years later, I'm still overwhelmed by the cross. It's the inspiration behind all that I do. It's the key to repenting and doing the things I know He's called me to. Not out of duty or religious guilt – but out of gratitude for what He did for me on that tree.

Remembering and repenting.

That's what we need to do if our love for Jesus has grown cold. So if that's you, here are some potential next steps to take that might help you in that journey.

Responding to Jesus' Letter (Part 1)

1) Reflect on the cross, and all that Jesus did for you there. Listen to *When I Survey the Wondrous Cross*, reminding yourself of His love, and allowing His Spirit to renew your love for Him.

2) Take a few minutes to remember and write down some of the things you used to do when your heart was full of gratitude for all that Jesus has done for you.

3) Once you have your list, ask yourself if you're still doing these things. If you're not, ask God if you need to be doing any of them. Commit yourself to do the ones you sense Him calling you to – not out of a need to justify yourself – but as a way to show Him love for all He's done for you.

Part 2: Loving People

> "Yet I hold this against you: you have forsaken the love you had at first."
> ~ Revelation 2:4

Jesus said it's impossible to truly love God without also loving people. They go together: "The greatest command is to love the Lord your God with all your heart, soul, and strength. And the second is like it: love your neighbor as yourself" (Matt 22:37). John, the author of Revelation, and pastor of the church at Ephesus, said the same thing: "If anyone says, 'I love God,' yet hates his brother, he is a liar" (1 John 4:19). In other words, if we claim to love God, but don't love people, there's a problem. Jesus says if this love problem doesn't get remedied, He will "remove our lamp stand" (2:5), which is code for "you'll no longer be part of My church."

That's how significant loving people is. Good works and right doctrine are important (and the church at Ephesus certainly had both), but that doesn't make up for a lack of love. This is where many Bible-believing churches in America parallel the church at Ephesus. Most have the reputation of fighting for the truth. And that's good. But do we also have the reputation of *loving each other so much that we're willing to lay down our lives for one another?*

The early church father, Tertullian, wrote that when the heathens of the second century peeked over the fence at the church, they would say, *"See how they love one another."*

Is that what people in our day say when they look at us?
Rarely.

Personal Confession

Early on in my walk with Jesus, I was not a very loving person. Passionate for the truth, yes; concerned about theology and doctrine, yes; loving, not as much. It's embarrassing to admit, but I remember actually saying, "I love God, but I just can't stand most people."

I still wince when I think about how those words came out of my mouth. But worse than those words coming out of my *mouth* is the fact that those words reflected an attitude coming out of my *heart*. And I justified my lack of love (especially for people who had offended me), on the basis that: "Hey, I believe the right things about God, and that's all that matters."

Jesus' letter to the church at Ephesus reminds us that is not all that matters. It's not enough to simply believe the right things about God. It's important, but it's not everything. J.I. Packer, a theologian who has written volumes about the importance of believing the right things about God, hit the nail on the head when he commented about how Evangelicals can smell unsound doctrine a mile away, and yet genuine love often proves rare among us.[10]

Ouch.

They Will Know We are Christians By our Love!

It's not enough for Christians to be doctrinally correct. Jesus is looking for more: "A new command I give you: Love one another. As I have loved you, so you must love one another. By this everyone will know that you are my disciples, if you love one another" (John 13:34-35).

Here's a multiple-choice question. Based on these verses from John 13, Jesus said the world would know that we are his disciples by what?

a) Our theological training and doctrinal correctness
b) Our willingness to call out sin
c) Our personal piety
d) Our good works
e) Our ***love*** for one another

Hint: if you're not sure of the correct answer, it's the bold, italicized and underlined option!

Don't misunderstand me. I'm not minimizing the importance of options a-d. Jesus is looking for those attributes, too. And according to the opening words of Christ's letter to the church at Ephesus, the believers had those characteristics. What the church was missing, though, was *the* one attribute that Jesus said is to be the distinguishing characteristic of His followers: LOVE!

A Case Study in Learning to Love

During my study of this letter, I was reminded that my journey of learning to love people has some similarities to that of the Apostle John. Like me, John began his spiritual journey with a lot of passion. And like me, he had some rough edges regarding his attitude toward people, especially those who offended him. Remember the nickname Jesus gave John?

"Son of Thunder" (Mark 3:17).

There was a reason Jesus gave John that nickname. One day, Jesus' disciples went into a Samaritan village to preach to them about the Kingdom of God. But the people there didn't want to listen. John's response was to ask Jesus to call down fire from heaven and torch them. Talk about a short fuse.

But by the grace of God, the love of Christ, and the power of the Spirit, John was transformed. He went from being a *son of thunder*, wanting to call down fire to torch people – to being a *shepherd,* constantly calling his flock to love each other:

- "Love one another" (1 John 3:11).
- "We have passed from death to life, because we love our brothers" (1 John 3:14).
- "If anyone says, 'I love God,' yet hates his brother, he is a liar" (1 John 4:19).

According to church tradition, toward the end of his life, the Roman Empire released John from prison on Patmos, and allowed him to go back to Ephesus. He was too old and feeble to get to church meetings anymore without the brothers carrying him.

And he wasn't able to preach full sermons anymore. But when John did speak to the church, he gave them the same message over and over again: "Little children, love one another. Little children, love one another."

John's life is an example of how Jesus can transform a proud, self-righteous heart into one characterized by a deep love for people. John went from being the 'Son of Thunder' to the 'Apostle of love.' Jesus can do that same work of transformation in us, too, if we'll let Him. But that transformation process begins with repenting, turning from our way of thinking and doing to God's way of thinking and doing. That's why Jesus calls us "to repent" (v5).

Self-Centeredness Inventory

Part of the repentance process means getting specific about those self-centered tendencies in us that are keeping us from loving people. And one of the ways to get specific is by doing an inventory. This is not a feel-good exercise, but I've found it helpful, because writing down my self-centered tendencies helps me to call them out, so I can then repent of them. After all, that is what Jesus calls us to do in this letter: repent (v5).

To give you an idea of what a personal inventory on self-centeredness might look like, here are some things I wrote down that have been obstacles to me loving people:

- Being too lazy to put forth the effort it takes to serve people sacrificially
- Allowing a spirit of individualism to isolate me from people
- Becoming easily irritated with people who annoy or frustrate me
- Being so focused on my schedule that there is no room for interruptions
- Valuing my own personal preferences over other people's wants or needs
- Bailing on people when they disappoint or offend me

Sadly, it didn't take long for me to come up with that list.

The more important question, though, is this: Once I've gotten honest about my selfish tendencies, what does it look like to repent of them, since that is what Jesus calls us to do?

For the sake of illustration, let me be transparent about three of the selfish tendencies that have sometimes kept me from loving people. And then I'll share what it's looked like for me to repent of them. Your selfish tendencies might be different than mine, but hopefully my transparency will help you connect the dots as to what your repentance needs to look like.

Selfish Tendency #1: Spirit of Individualism/Isolation

By nature, I'm an introvert. Contrary to some extroverts, though, being an introvert is not a sin! It just means I recharge my emotional batteries alone. Big groups tend to drain me, especially in settings where I'm expected to interact with lots of people. But the Lord has helped me. One of the things I'm grateful for (as an introvert pastor) is that being in this role has allowed me to experience God's strength, empowering me to do what I'm not naturally wired to do.

I used to wish I was an extrovert. I would answer personality tests in a way that made them say I was an extrovert, so I would be a "good fit" for the pastoral role. I've come to realize, though, that's not how God made me. I've learned to be okay with being an introvert. But there is a dark side for introverts. Sometimes we use our personality temperament as an excuse to isolate ourselves. But how can I really love people if I'm avoiding people? I can't.

Here is what repentance looks like for me. It begins with reminding myself of the gospel: that Jesus didn't avoid me by staying in the cozy confines of Heaven. He came to Earth. He drew close to me, demonstrating His love through the incarnation (John 1:14) and the cross (Rom 5:8). And the more I think about that, the more inspired I am to love others in response to His love for me.

One practical way I've grown in loving people is through following my wife's lead. Amanda encourages us to put ourselves in settings where we can love people – whether it's hosting a small group, having people over to our home for a meal, or serving those in need. Her heart for hospitality has been a significant means of God curbing my tendency to isolate myself. So what's my advice? Find someone who really values community and people, and marry them!

If that's not in the cards for you – lean into community, join a small group, or find ways to pour yourself into others. Not that every waking moment of the day needs to be spent with people. Even Jesus took time to get away from the disciples. But look at your calendar and ask yourself if it reflects a life that is investing in people. Every few weeks, Amanda and I sit down with our calendar to choose specific times when we will get together with people to serve and encourage them. Amanda would probably choose to do more of this, but she knows that filling all of our evenings would be very draining for me. She's sensitive to my introvert wiring. At the same time, her gift of hospitality has helped pull me up and away from an individualistic life, and into settings where I'm in a position to really love people.

Full disclosure: I still don't look forward to hosting opportunities with the same excitement as Amanda. I probably never will. But every time we have people over to share a meal, or play games, or pray together, I'm genuinely glad we did. Not only is it a blessing to others; it ends up blessing me, too. That makes sense. After all, God made me to love people. There is joy that comes when we are aligned with the purpose for which He created us.

For what it's worth, leaning into community and being intentional about relationships isn't just good for your soul. According to the data, it's good for your body, too. John Ortberg cites one such research project, called the Alameda County Study:

> Headed by a Harvard social scientist, it tracked the lives of 7,000 people over nine years. Researchers found that the most isolated people were three times more *likely to die* than those with strong relational connections. People who had bad health habits (such as smoking, poor eating,

obesity or alcohol use) but strong social ties lived *significantly longer* than people who had great health habits but were isolated. In other words, it is better to eat Twinkies with good friends than to eat broccoli alone. Harvard researcher Robert Putnam notes that if you belong to no groups but decide to join one, 'you cut your risk of dying over the next year *in half.*'[11]

This study was the inspiration for our church's small group campaign: "Join a small group, or die!"

Jokes aside, God made us for community. He made us for relationships. He made us to love people. Some of us, like me, just need to stop making excuses and be more intentional about it. Perhaps calendarizing this value will help you start moving in that direction.

Selfish Tendency #2: Becoming Easily Irritated

Do you ever get annoyed or irritated when you're around certain people? Maybe a co-worker? Maybe a family member? Maybe someone in your small group or church? I'm sure we can all think of someone. What is it about them that irritates you? Or perhaps the better question is: what is it about *you* that makes you get so irritated with them?

Here's what I'm realizing about my tendency to get irritated with people: it often stems from my own pride and self-righteousness. I try to rationalize that my frustration is the result of the words and actions of someone else. And there is probably some truth to that. But my irritation is ultimately my problem. It's a symptom of an elevated view of myself, and a failure to remember that Jesus was willing to go to the cross for my sins. After all, how can I become so quickly irritated with the sins and shortcomings of others when I consider what Jesus was willing to do to save me from mine?

Here's what repentance looks like for me in those moments when I slip into becoming irritated with someone: I go back to the gospel. I ask God to help me view this person through the lens of what Jesus did for *me* while *I* was sinning against Him. My sins didn't just irritate Jesus; they drove the nails into His hands and feet. When I stop and reflect on that, how can I not be more patient with that person who is irritating me? I don't do this perfectly. Not even close. But I'm learning to turn my gaze to the cross when I'm tempted to be irritated, annoyed or offended, so that He can grow in me a love I didn't know was possible.

Selfish Tendency #3: Bailing Easily on Relationships

In our culture, if you shop at a grocery store, and they change the way they sell produce, and you don't like it, you just start shopping somewhere else. You don't feel guilty about leaving one store to shop somewhere else. That's the nature of shopping in our consumeristic society. The customer is always right. Shop wherever they give you what you want.

Unfortunately, some of us have allowed this consumer way of thinking to infect the way we view the church and the people God has placed in our lives. We live in a culture that is more and more marked by self-centeredness and short fuses. Someone says something that hurts our feelings, or posts something online that offends us – and we write them off, or unfriend them. And we feel absolutely justified in doing so.

But how do we reconcile this as followers of the One who sacrificially gave Himself for us, despite all the times we've offended Him? Shouldn't we resemble Him in the way we patiently endure the people He's put in our lives?

Let me be clear, there are times when it's right to break off a relationship. If someone is cheating on you, you're not bound to stay with that person. If your pastor starts teaching things that are heretical, run for the door and find a church that preaches God's Word. If a friend repeatedly tempts you in ways that are leading you to be unfaithful to Jesus, it's probably time to find some new friends. There are times when the Holy Spirit calls us to move on. But the tendency, for most of us in this culture, is to bail prematurely.

JESUS' WORD TO THE CHURCH AT EPHESUS: LOVE

I've been the chief of sinners on this one, especially in the early days of my walk with Christ. If you offended me, I was done with you. I had a short fuse, and a long memory. And I justified this pattern of bailing on the basis that: "Hey, I'm right and you're wrong, and that's all that matters." According to Jesus' word to the church at Ephesus, though, that's not all that matters. Truth is important. But so is love.

I believe this is one of the reasons God has placed me in pastoral ministry these twenty plus years: to teach me how to love people over the long haul. As I look back over the years of serving in His church, there are many people I would have bailed on, except that, because I was their pastor, it would have been difficult to do so. I worshiped with them every Sunday. I served beside them during the week. I couldn't outright reject them without creating awkwardness for myself.

As a result of needing to work through the offense, *I* am the one who is truly the better for the relationships I now have with these people. By His grace, God has used my selfishness (of not wanting to create awkwardness for myself) to show me that the people I would have bailed on, have incredible gifts to share with me and the body of Christ. I've experienced this over and over again, simply because I stayed in relationship long enough to see past an offense. Thankfully, other believers have been gracious in doing the same with me, seeing past the times when *I've* hurt or offended them.

Amanda is one of my inspirations in relational perseverance. Whenever there is an offense or a rift with another believer, she has a mantra: "We're going to be in Heaven together forever. We might as well figure out how to love each other now." It's amazing how often I think about this when a fellow believer has offended me, and I'm tempted to bail on them. And it works. It puts a temporary offense in an eternal context, and motivates me to love them like Jesus loved me.

Loving God. Loving people. Jesus said this is the greatest command.

Jesus, teach us how to love.

Responding to Jesus' Letter

Take a few minutes to do some inventory on the following questions:

1) What self-centered tendencies are you prone to let get in the way of loving people?

    - Individualism?
    - Laziness?
    - Being too easily irritated?
    - Being too focused on your own plans or schedule?
    - Personal comfort being your highest goal?
    - A tendency to bail when someone has offended or hurt you?
    - Something else?

    a) Name it. Get specific and then confess it:
    _____

    b) Repent of it, asking God for His forgiveness (for the past) and His help to guard against it (in the future), so that you can better love the people He's calling you to love.

2) Is there a specific person in your life who is difficult for you to love? If so, then:

    a) Pray: "Jesus, help me view _____ through the lens of the cross, the way You loved me, despite my sin."

    b) Ask the Holy Spirit if there are any specific ways He would have you love this person.

Digging Deeper

1) Read *The Cross of Christ* (by John Stott), a book about what was happening on that blood-stained patch of real estate, called Calvary. But be careful in picking up this book. It just might change your life, like it changed mine!

2) Read *Life Together* (by Dietrich Bonhoeffer), the most influential book I've ever read on Christian community. It serves as both a prophetic rebuke to our individualistic culture, and an exhortation to those who really want to love others in the church like Jesus calls us to.

3) Read *Everybody's Normal Til You Get to Know Them* (by John Ortberg), a wonderfully practical book that outlines the pitfalls of relationships (because of our sin and ignorance), and gives sage advice about how to love people in a way that reflects the love of Christ.

3

JESUS' WORD TO THE CHURCH AT SMYRNA: COURAGE

POLYCARP IS ONE OF MY HEROES.

A disciple of the Apostle John, he was pastor of the church at Smyrna in the early second century. His story not only provides a glimpse into the persecution the believers in Smyrna faced. It also illustrates the courage that characterized them.

At nearly ninety years old, Polycarp was summoned by the Roman authorities, and called upon to renounce his faith in Christ. He refused. As a result, he was led to a crowded stadium and given one final opportunity to deny Christ. "Confess that Caesar is Lord, and we'll set you free," the authorities demanded.

The old man looked at them in horror and replied, "Eighty years have I served Christ and He never did me any wrong. How can I blaspheme my King and my Savior?"

Polycarp was further threatened, but refused to recant. In fact, he grew more resolved: "Since you are vainly urgent that I should swear by the fortunes of Caesar and pretend not to know who or what I am, here may I declare with boldness that I am a Christian."

The authorities were furious, "We have wild beasts at our disposal and we will cast you to them, unless you repent." But the old man remained steadfast and unmoved by their threats. Finally, they warned Polycarp: "If you don't recant, we will burn you at the stake." To which Polycarp replied, "You threaten me with fire which burns for an hour and then is extinguished, but you are ignorant of the fire of the coming eternal judgment that is reserved for the ungodly. What are you waiting for? Bring forth what you will."

Polycarp was then burned at the stake for his faith in Christ.[12]

That's what happened to the pastor of the church at Smyrna, the same church, which years earlier, had received a letter from Jesus, encouraging them to not be afraid of the coming persecution. Polycarp's testimony is evidence that Jesus' word really did prepare them (and their pastor) not to give into fear.

This letter can do that for us, too. We may not have to face the kind of persecution the church at Smyrna faced. But this letter can transform the way we face our fears: of rejection, financial loss, failure, people not liking us, and a thousand other fears. This letter can prepare us to courageously face whatever hardships this world may throw at us.

So if you're in need of a good dose of COURAGE, this letter is for you.

> "To the angel of the church in Smyrna write: These are the words of Him who is the First and the Last, who died and came to life again. I know your afflictions and your poverty – yet you are rich! I know the slander of those who say they are Jews and are not, but are a synagogue of Satan. Do not be afraid of what you are about to suffer. I tell you, the devil will put some of you in prison to test you, and you will suffer persecution for ten days. Be faithful, even to the point of death, and I will give you the crown of life. He who has ears, let him hear what the Spirit says to the churches. He who overcomes will not be hurt at all by the second death."
> ~ Revelation 2:8-11

JESUS' WORD TO THE CHURCH AT SMYRNA: COURAGE

Historical Context

It's impossible to fully grasp the challenges facing the believers in Smyrna without first understanding the Imperial Cult. The Imperial Cult was the state religion that mandated everyone living within the borders of the Roman Empire worship the emperor. Those who refused were imprisoned or executed.

There was, however, one group of people who received an exemption from having to worship the emperor: the Jews. Over the course of decades of ruling the Jewish people, the Romans realized they were never going to get them to worship Caesar, no matter the punishment.

Rome knew they had to either kill every Jew in the Empire, or give them an exemption. Rome decided to grant an exemption. But there were conditions. In exchange for their religious freedom, the Jewish leaders had to promise Rome that they would never undermine the emperor's authority by calling anyone else their king. If Rome ever caught wind that the Jews were giving their allegiance to someone besides Caesar, the Empire would revoke their religious freedom, destroy their synagogues, and execute them for treason. But as long as the Jews didn't call anyone other than Caesar their king, they could enjoy this exemption.

What did this exemption for the Jews have to do with the Christians?

In the first century, Christianity was primarily a movement *within* Judaism. Most first century Jews, who became Christians, still understood themselves to be Jews: Messianic Jews. They attended synagogue. They listened to the reading of the Old Testament Scriptures. But they also believed the Scriptural prophecies about the Messiah had been fulfilled in Jesus. Therefore they confessed Jesus as Lord and King, titles reserved for Caesar. As you can imagine, this created a problem for the Christians, not only with Rome, but also with the Jewish synagogue leaders.

Most synagogue leaders were nervous about how the Jesus movement might affect their exemption clause. After all, they had worked hard to obtain their religious freedom. They didn't want to risk losing it by being associated with these Christians, who were proclaiming Jesus to be Lord and King. And so the synagogue leaders began distancing themselves from the Jesus followers by slandering them and kicking them out of the synagogue. Why? To show Rome that their political loyalties remained with the emperor. It was to these synagogue leaders that Jesus is referring when He says: "I know the *slander* of those who say they are Jews and are not, but are a synagogue of Satan" (v9).

The reason it was so devastating for Christians to be ex-communicated from the synagogue was because there was, then, no way to escape the imperial mandate of worshiping the emperor. Once the synagogue leaders didn't accept the Christians as Jews, they no longer qualified for the exemption. That meant Rome would then come after them, and force them to confess, 'Caesar is Lord,' or execute them for treason if they refused. The believers in Smyrna were between a rock and a hard place.

From the Jewish authorities, they faced <u>ex-communication</u> if they confessed Jesus as Lord.

From the Roman authorities, they faced <u>execution</u> if they didn't confess Caesar as Lord.

If I had been a Christian in Smyrna, I think I would have been tempted to be quiet about my faith in Jesus. You know, worship God and attend synagogue, but believe in Jesus *in my heart*, holding back from declaring, "Jesus is Lord," so I could stay under the radar, and continue to benefit from the synagogue exemption clause.

What's so remarkable about the believers in Smyrna, though, is that they weren't shying away from declaring their faith in Jesus. They weren't holding back from talking about Jesus. Despite the opposition, they were boldly proclaiming Jesus' Lordship, and faithfully enduring the consequences. In fact, Smyrna was just one of two churches that didn't receive any words of rebuke from Jesus. They suffered greatly, but not because they had done anything wrong.

Suffering Doesn't Mean God has Abandoned You

If this church had been so faithful, then why did Jesus need to send them a letter?

Some people believe the only time God wants to speak to us is if He needs to correct us or give us a spiritual spanking. Not true. Jesus didn't need to rebuke the believers at Smyrna. But He still wanted to send them a letter – to encourage them, and to speak into their pain with perspective that would revolutionize the way they viewed their suffering.

Jesus, at the very outset of this letter, lets the church know that He is aware of their suffering. He is not some distant Deity, ignorant or apathetic about what they're experiencing. Jesus knows exactly what they're going through. That's why, after introducing Himself, the first two words Jesus says to this church are: "I know…" (v9).

"I *know* your afflictions and your poverty," Jesus says.

He knows all about their hardships. And so He can speak to their hearts, not with trite clichés or religious jargon, but with exactly what they need to hear: straight-up truth about suffering.

Jesus wants to do the same with us.

One of the reasons this letter is so important for American believers is because most of us don't know how to view our suffering. We don't know how to endure our suffering. Ours is a culture that has latched onto all kinds of coping mechanisms to try deal with our pain: alcohol, drugs, pornography, sex, shopping, social media, binge eating, gambling. We have an ever increasing number of addictions we indulge in to try to deal with our pain, boredom or loneliness.

Sadly, believers are not that different from the rest of the culture on this point. And that's because so many of us have bought into the lie that if we have Jesus in our life, we won't suffer, or shouldn't suffer. And then when suffering does come our way, we're completely caught off guard, even wondering if God has abandoned us.

I've lost count of how many people I've talked to over the years, who have confided in me that they don't understand why life is so hard for them *even though they believe in Jesus.* They don't know how to reconcile the pain of life with their faith in Jesus. Frequently, the reason they're so confused is because the version of Christianity they signed on to was one that promised them that following Jesus would make their life *easier.* Jesus, though, never promised His followers an *easy* life.

> Jesus said, *If you want to be my disciple, deny yourself.*
> Jesus said, *Take up your cross, and follow Me.*
> Jesus said, *If you want to save your life, you must lose it.* 13

Don't misunderstand the invitation: following Jesus is not a call to a sad, sour, somber life. To follow Jesus is to be part of the most amazing movement on Earth – one marked by peace, joy, forgiveness, the presence and power of God, and the hope of Heaven!

But Jesus also said there would be pain and suffering in this life – before we enter into that eternal Kingdom that's coming. His first followers knew this. In Acts 14:22, when Paul was preaching to a group of new believers, he didn't pull any punches. He told them flat out: "We *must* go through many hardships to enter the Kingdom of God."

Many of us missed that part of the message when we said 'yes' to Jesus. That's why so many of us are confused about the pain and the suffering of our lives. We think God has abandoned us, when in reality, this is precisely what Jesus said would happen.

Followers of Jesus in other cultures understand suffering better than we do. For example, Chinese house church leaders actually refer to persecution and prison as their *seminary.* It's where their future pastors are trained for leadership. In fact, Chinese believers are hesitant to appoint anyone to leadership who has not been to the "seminary of prison!"

What would happen if we saw our suffering, not as a sign of God's abandonment, but as a training ground for ministry leadership and service in His Kingdom?

Don't Be Afraid!

Jesus wanted more for the church at Smyrna than for them to survive. He wanted them to thrive *without fear*. That's why, in the next verse, Jesus tells them, "Don't be afraid." It's not unusual for God to tell His people not to fear. This command is found throughout the Bible. What's surprising in this letter is what follows the command. Jesus says: "Don't be afraid" (v10a), and then He previews the scary things coming their way – things that would cause most of us to be very afraid: "suffering, prison, persecution, and death" (v10b).

Is Jesus serious? Does he really think the way to inspire courage is by telling us that suffering, prison, persecution, and death are coming our way? That doesn't seem like a very effective strategy for quelling fear! It's not the strategy I've used with my children. As a dad, when I tell my children not to be afraid of something, I usually follow it up by explaining to them that what they're afraid of is *not* likely to happen. For example, when my girls were little, they were afraid of the White Witch of Narnia. At night, they were scared that she would sneak into our house and turn them into stone. Of course, I knew that no white witch was going to break in and turn them into stone, so I would reassure them by saying, "You don't need to be afraid, *because that's not going to happen.*"

But 'that's not going to happen' isn't the basis for Jesus telling His children in Smyrna not to be afraid. Instead, Jesus tells the church at Smyrna to look squarely into the face of suffering that *is* coming their way, and still He says, "Don't be afraid."

Evidently, Jesus' primary goal is not to keep us physically safe. If it was, here's what His letter would have said:

> "To the church at Smyrna write: I'm so sorry about these afflictions. But don't worry. Never again will

you have to face pain, hardship or suffering of any kind. I'll keep you physically safe from now on. And I won't ask you to do anything scary or outside your comfort zone ever again. From now on, I'll just give you a nice, cozy existence here on Earth until I take you to Heaven."

That's what Sky Fairy Jesus would have said. But what Real Jesus says is:

> "I know about your afflictions…Be faithful, even to the point of death."
> ~ Revelation 2:9, 10

Some of us wonder how Jesus could say this to people who were already suffering so much. But that's because some of us have a distorted view of Jesus, as someone whose agenda is to sprinkle feel-good pixy dust on us to protect us from bad things ever happening. But Jesus never promises a life where bad things won't happen to us. What He promises is a life where we can be *free from the paralyzing fear* of those bad things that may happen to us.

I'm writing this chapter from a rural village in East Africa, where our family is helping to re-launch a pastoral training school. Our security at night consists of two watchmen with spears. Together, the guards weigh about 220 pounds, soaking wet. If there are bandits in the area, we hope our watchmen will be awake, and that the thieves trying to break in won't have guns. There is no 911 to call, no local police to come to our aid if something bad happens. We're trusting the Lord with our lives, but that doesn't mean bad things can't happen to us out here. Last month, the other missionary family in our village had someone attempt to break into their home in the middle of the night. Fortunately, their watchmen were awake and stopped it. But that's not always the story. Last week, three elderly nuns were raped and brutally murdered in their convent, sixty miles from where we're living.

Bad things happen all the time.

We live in a fallen world. Until Jesus returns and sets it to rights, terrible things will continue to happen, even to those who love Him and have put their trust in Him. So to tell my kids, "Nothing bad will happen," isn't just wishful thinking; it communicates something about God that isn't true: that His primary concern is to keep us *safe*.

The truth is: Jesus never promises a life where bad things won't happen to us. Rather, Jesus promises a life where we can be *free from the paralyzing fear* of those bad things that may happen to us. Jesus came to set us free from all of our fears:

- Our fear of pain
- Our fear of rejection
- Our fear of financial loss
- Our fear of people not liking us
- Our fear of being alone
- Our fear of failure
- And a thousand other fears that paralyze us from following Him

So how is it that Jesus can set us free from all of these fears? Because He already faced and defeated the ultimate fear that's at the root of every one of our lesser fears: Death!

The Bookends of the Letter: Death

That's the reason Jesus introduces himself the way he does in this letter: "These are the words of Him who is the First and the Last, who died and came to life again" (v8). If Jesus, our King, rose from the dead, then what is there to fear? Nothing. Not even death. And to reinforce this truth, Jesus concludes the letter with: "Be faithful, even to the point of death, and I will give you the crown of life… The one who is victorious will not be hurt at all by the second death!" (v10b).

Jesus doesn't soften the message about our impending death. He tells us it's coming. And that's not just true for the Smyrna believers. It's true for all of us. After all, the death rate, even among Christians, is still holding steady at 100%. There's no need to be afraid, though. Because of Christ's victory over the grave, the second death, the one that brings an eternal sting, has been swallowed up. It can't hurt us. We can now look squarely into the face of whatever suffering might come our way, and hear Jesus declaring: "I've defeated death. My resurrection presence is now with you in such a powerful way – that even in the midst of danger, pain, or death, you don't have to be afraid anymore!"

Jesus doesn't bookend this letter with "death" because He's trying to be morbid. He's trying to give us eternal perspective, the kind that sets us free from all our fears.

Die Up Front!

There's a step we need to take, though, before we can be free of our fears: Die.Up.Front.

What does that mean? Let me start with what dying up front is not. It's not about going out and looking for suffering – to "prove" to God how serious I am about following Him. I don't get bonus points with God by seeking out something difficult, dangerous, or deadly.

Dying up front is simply settling in my mind that I will follow Jesus no matter what, even if my life doesn't play out like I want it to, even if my life is marked by suffering and disappointment.

Here is why this is such an important step to take. Once we come to that place where we're willing to say: "Jesus, I will obey You no matter what happens to me" – there is nothing Satan can throw at us to hi-jack our obedience to God. Nothing. Not disappointment. Not pain. Not suffering. Not even the threat of death.

That's part of the reason Jesus previews for the church at Smyrna that persecution and death were coming their way. He was giving them the opportunity to die up front, so they could abandon themselves to Him, choosing to follow Him no matter

JESUS' WORD TO THE CHURCH AT SMYRNA: COURAGE

what Rome or the religious leaders might do to them. And it worked, as illustrated by the courage of their pastor, Polycarp.

Jesus is calling us to this same step. He's inviting us to die up front, too, so that our fears will no longer hold us back from following Him wherever He leads. Now, that doesn't mean we need to go jumping out of an airplane without a parachute. It means being willing to do whatever He calls us to. Let's not confuse foolish risk-taking with courageous obedience. There's a difference.

There's a fictional story about a man who, upon dying, appears at the pearly gates, where Saint Peter greets him and asks him, *"Have you ever done anything noble – to merit getting into Heaven?"* (The idea that we get into Heaven by our good works is also fictional – but for the sake of the story, indulge in some bad theology!)

The man responds to Peter's question by saying: "Well, I can think of one noble thing. Once I came upon a gang of bikers who were threatening a young woman. I told them to leave her alone, but they wouldn't listen. So I approached the largest and most heavily tattooed biker. I smacked him on the head, kicked his bike over, ripped out his nose ring and threw it on the ground, and told him, 'Leave her alone now or you'll answer to me.'"

Saint Peter was impressed. "Wow, when did this happen?" he asked.

To which the man replied, "Just a couple of minutes ago."[14]

Let's not confuse the courage to face suffering with foolishly going out and *looking* for it. As Oswald Chambers writes: "Choosing to suffer means that there must be something wrong with you, but choosing God's will – even if it means you will suffer – is something very different. No normal, healthy saint ever chooses suffering; he simply chooses God's will, just as Jesus did, whether it means suffering or not."[15]

Dying up front is about settling in my mind that I will follow Jesus no matter what, even if my life doesn't play out like I want it to. Dying up front is about coming to this place where I say, "Jesus, Your sacrifice on the cross is so amazing, Your forgiveness is so undeserved, and Your coming Kingdom is so glorious – that my obedience to You is on the table without any conditions or strings, even if it means I have to endure pain and hardship for the rest of my life."

A Case Study in Dying Up Front

Believers in the underground church in China understand what it is to die up front. Like the state religion of the Roman Empire, the government in China doesn't want any religion competing for the allegiance they believe belongs to them alone. They've even gone so far as to imprison and kill Christians who preach Jesus. Ironically, though, it's not the Chinese believers who live in fear; it's the government officials who are often the ones undone by the courage of Christians. Nik Ripken interviewed a group of believers in China, asking them how this happens. They offered this scenario as an explanation:

> The security police regularly harass believers who own the property where a house-church meets. The police say, 'You have got to stop these meetings! If you do not stop these meetings, we will confiscate your house, and we will throw you out into the street.' Then the [Christian] property owners will respond, 'Do you want my house? Do you want my farm? Well, if you do, then you need to talk to Jesus because I gave this property to Him.'
>
> The security police will not know what to make of that answer. So they will say, 'We don't have any way to get to Jesus, but we can certainly get to you! When we take your property, you and your family will have nowhere to live!' At which point the house-church believers will declare, 'Then we will be free to trust God for shelter as well as for our daily bread.'

'If you keep this up, we will beat you!' the persecutors will tell them. 'Then we will be free to trust Jesus for healing,' the believers will respond.

'Then we will put you in prison!' the police will threaten. By now, the believers' response is almost predictable: 'Then we will be free to preach the good news of Jesus to the captives, to set them free. We will be free to plant churches in prison.'

'If you try to do that we will kill you!' the frustrated authorities will vow. And, with utter consistency, the house-church believers will reply, 'Then we will be free to go to heaven and be with Jesus forever.'[16]

That's the kind of 'dying up front' step Jesus is inviting us to take – so that we might be free to go all in with Him. As Erwin McManus says: "Jesus' death wasn't to free us from dying, but to free us from the fear of death. Jesus came to liberate us so that we could die up front and then live. *Jesus Christ wants to take us to places where only dead men and women can go.*"[17]

God has incredible plans for us, but we won't be able to step into them until we die up front, until we completely abandon our lives and relinquish our expectations into Jesus' hands. Only then will we experience the life He came to bring us. This is what Jesus was driving at when He said, "Whoever wants to save his life will lose it, but whoever loses his life for Me will find it" (Matthew 16:25).

Is This Letter Really For Me?

Maybe you're wondering: Okay, but how do I apply the words of this 1,900 year old letter to my everyday life? After all, I'm not experiencing the kind of persecution and suffering that the believers in Smyrna were facing. True. But even if we're not facing the same hardships, there are places in our lives where we are afraid or anxious. And Jesus wants to set us free from *every* fear that's holding us back. And He wants to do it *today*. Before that can happen, though, we need to get honest about where fear has its grip on us. So let's name our fears. What are you afraid of? What are you nervous about? What causes you anxiety?

- Sharing your faith
- Having enough money
- What people think about you
- Letting people see your sins and shortcomings
- The future
- Serving in the church – because you feel inadequate
- Parenting challenges
- Dentist/doctor visits
- Being rejected
- The political situation of our world
- Getting out of your comfort zone
- Illness/disease/sickness
- Failure (as a parent, as a spouse, in school, in your job, etc.)
- Being alone
- Physical pain
- Confronting someone you know you need to talk to
- Going on a mission trip overseas
- Disappointing people
- Speaking in public
- Entrusting a dream or a hope to Jesus
- Giving/tithing
- Letting go of something you need to let go of
- Something else: _____

Identify one place in your life where fear or anxiety is robbing you of peace, or holding you back from taking a step you need to take. Once you've identified your fear or that challenging thing God is calling you to, write it down:

Jesus, I confess I'm afraid of _____

Once we've gotten honest about our fears, we're ready for the all-important step of 'dying up front.' Let me illustrate what this looks like by way of an exercise I did during my study of this letter. Basically, I did my own personal audit of those places in life where fear has had its grip on me. That list is too long for me to share it in its entirety, so I'll just share three of the bigger fears I've wrestled with in my life. Your fears will be different, but the principle of 'dying up front' can be applied regardless of the specifics. Hopefully by illustrating what 'dying up front' has looked like in my life, it'll shed light on what 'dying up front' might look like in yours.

Fear #1: What If I Never Find a Wife/Girlfriend?

Throughout high school and college, this fear was huge, although I never admitted it. I tried to play it cool and act as if I didn't really want a girlfriend – which was a perfect cover, since I didn't have one. Prior to meeting Amanda, I had never really had a serious girlfriend. There was one girl I had dated in high school, but that relationship was short-lived, before I heard those infamous words, "I just want to be friends."

In college, when I got serious about following Jesus, there were plenty of Christian girls I liked. I just couldn't get any of them to like me back. I was even at a Christian school, where the on-campus ratio of girls to guys was three to one. You would think that would have helped my cause, but still, for the first three years of college, I could not get a girlfriend! There may have been a lot of reasons for that, but that's a subject for another day. The point I'm driving at is this: not being able to get a girlfriend became a source of disappointment and anxiety. Ultimately, it became a test. And the test was this: *Would my desire for a girlfriend/wife move me to compromise, settling for something less than I knew would honor God – out of fear of missing out on something I really wanted?*

I realize the irony of confessing this fear when I've now been married to my beautiful bride for over twenty years. But I didn't know the way my story would unfold during that season of disappointment. And that's the point: *we don't know how things will turn out this side of heaven.*

I understand why well-meaning Christians tell young people: "God has someone perfect picked out for you." Some say it to inspire patience. Some say it as an encouragement not to compromise or settle. Some say it to try to comfort those who are lonely or longing for companionship. But many say it because they actually believe God has a soul mate picked out for every one of us. We do realize, though, God never says this anywhere in His Word, right? Trust me, I've looked for that verse; it's not there!

Finally, there came a point in college when I sensed the Lord calling me to stop holding on so tightly to my dream of having a girlfriend or getting married. It was not easy. I didn't want to let go. But after some initial resistance, I finally came to this place where I was willing to 'die up front.' I didn't use that terminology back then, but that's what happened. I came to terms with the possibility that I may never get married. And I told Jesus – if that was my story – I was committed to following Him anyway.

And then the strangest thing happened: I really was okay. Fear of being single my whole life was replaced with peace that Jesus is enough. Don't misunderstand me: I didn't rule out getting married. And it's not like I stopped talking to girls. In fact, as cliché as it sounds, it was soon after coming to this place of surrender that I met Amanda. Now, I'm not suggesting that the secret to getting a girlfriend is to be okay with not having a girlfriend – as if it's some reverse psychology trick we're playing on God. No, dying up front regarding my dream of "getting a girlfriend" was simply a means of letting God get a hold of more of my heart, and moving me to a place where I was resolved to follow Him, *even if His plan for me didn't include marriage.*

Fear #2: What If My Children Choose Not To Follow Jesus?

After I got married, I was afraid to have kids. Not because of diapers or toddler tantrums or sleepless nights. Okay, I was a little bit afraid of those! Even more, though, I was afraid of the pain

I would feel if my children chose not to follow Jesus. And yes, I know Proverbs 22:6–"Train up a child in the way he should go, and when he is old he will not turn from it." I also know why well-meaning Christians quote this verse. We do so to remind each other that doing the work of teaching our children about Jesus is the right way to parent them; and that generally speaking, godly parenting grows godly children. But this Scripture is a *proverb*, not a *guarantee*. There are no guarantees that if we train our children in the Lord they won't still go their own way. I've been a pastor long enough to see this happen with lots of godly parents.

Even though all four of our kids love Jesus today, this is still a fear that periodically creeps into my heart, and tempts me to drift toward worry. My guess is that I will periodically feel this fear with grandchildren, too. So for me, 'dying up front' means giving up the guarantee. I'm still called to be diligent in loving my children and pointing them to Jesus. I'm still trusting that God's sovereign purposes will be worked out in their lives. But instead of trying to find the silver bullet that insures that my kids (and future grandchildren) will always follow Jesus, God has called me to look squarely into the face of my fear and hear Him say over it, 'Don't be afraid. Love your children. But remember that I love them more than you do. Train them. Point them to Me. But then entrust them to Me. Stop living in fear of something you can't control.'

Fear #3: But God, I'm Afraid To Speak In Public!

For as far back as I can remember I was afraid of speaking in front of people. I didn't even like doing 'show and tell' in grade school. I hated giving presentations in middle school and high school. I even dropped out of my public speaking class in college because I didn't want to give a five-minute speech in front of twenty other students. And this was *after* I sensed God calling me into full-time vocational ministry. That's when it hit me: I realized that speaking in front of people was a fear I was going to have to face. Here's what 'dying up front' looked like for me: I signed on to a summer internship with an inner-city ministry in Detroit, with a pastor who had a reputation for pushing interns *out of their comfort zone.*

It was brutal.

Why would I choose to do something I knew would be such a painful experience? Because I finally acknowledged that my fear of public speaking was going to paralyze me from doing what God wanted me to do, unless I did something drastic. Signing up to do that internship was exactly the kind of "dying up front" step I needed to take.

That summer internship involved being part of a team that did neighborhood evangelism events. Typically, the "real" pastors gave the gospel presentations at these gatherings. But one afternoon, about fifteen minutes before the program was to begin, the pastor turned to me, the lowly intern, and said, "You're going to give the message today." I was petrified. But there was no point in resisting. There was no way to wiggle out of it. I couldn't run home, tail between my legs. My home that summer was the pastor's basement! I had to do it. I had to face my fear of public speaking. So I did. And I know for a fact that at least one kid's life was changed that day: mine.

That day, I realized just because I *felt* afraid to do something didn't mean God couldn't help me do it. I discovered that even if I still *felt* afraid, I no longer had to be paralyzed by fear.

We Don't Have to Be Ruled By Our Feelings

Truth be told, I still sometimes get anxious before stepping up to speak in front of a group of people. I don't feel guilty about it, though. It's not a sin to *feel* afraid. It's part of being human. In fact, an article in the *New York Times Magazine* cited research that indicates some people actually have a genetic predisposition toward fear and anxiety. They've even located the gene: the slc6a4 gene on chromosome 17q12. People who are born with a short version of this gene are more likely to be afraid than people who are born with a long version of it. John Ortberg likes to ferret out

JESUS' WORD TO THE CHURCH AT SMYRNA: COURAGE

the real worry-warts by asking: "Now that you know about this fear gene, how many of you are *afraid* you might have the short version of it?"[18]

Here's the deal: you may have the short version of the slc6a4 gene, which predisposes you to be more susceptible to fear and anxiety. I do. Who cares! After all, here's what I've learned: having the short version of this gene does not determine how I have to live.

I wonder if this is why Jesus doesn't immediately set us free from all of our feelings of fear. He could. And sometimes He does. But what He always does – if we're willing to put our trust in Him and die up front – is set us free from being *paralyzed* by our feelings of fear. In other words, our feelings of fear might remain for a while, but we don't have to be ruled by them any longer. We can do what God calls us to do. We can face what we're called to face. And over time, as we do the things He's called us to do (despite our fears), our feelings of fear will typically diminish.

For example, I've been preaching now for over twenty years. But it's only in the last several that I've stopped waking up every Sunday feeling like I was going to throw up from nerves. That's what I used to experience every Sunday morning. Even though God did something in me (back in Detroit) to set me free from the *paralyzing* fear of public speaking – that didn't mean I would never *feel* fear again. But what God taught me during that internship was that I can now look squarely into the face of my fears, and do what He's called me to, *regardless of my feelings*.

Satan has duped so many of us into believing that as long as we're still feeling fear, we're stuck. And so we keep praying for God to take away our fears *so that* we can obey Him, instead of praying for the courage to obey Him *while* we're still afraid. Perhaps that's the prayer God is looking to answer. If you're a Christ-follower, the same Spirit who raised Jesus from the dead dwells within you, and His power trumps your genetic predisposition toward fear. Sure, it's a miracle when Jesus takes *away* our feelings of fear. But it's even more miraculous when He enables us to obey Him *while* we're afraid. That's real Spirit-inspired courage!

Walking Through the Doorway of our Fears

Facing our fears also opens us up to experience God's presence in a powerful way. Do we want to experience more of God? Perhaps facing our fears is one of the ways through which God is waiting to reveal Himself to us. As Erwin McManus says, "The door we fear going through the most may be the very one where we will meet God most profoundly."[19]

One of the surest ways to experience more of God's presence is by stepping through whatever door you're afraid of walking through – into whatever assignment you're afraid of taking on. I've certainly experienced that in my life. I can't even count all the times I've grown in my relationship with God by walking through some doorway I was afraid to walk through:

- The Doorway of Sharing my Faith (facing my fear of rejection)
- The Doorway of Confession (facing my fear of embarrassment)
- The Doorway of Risking Something for God (facing my fear of failure)
- The Doorway of Tithing (facing my fear of not having enough money)
- The Doorway of Serving in Rural East Africa (facing my fear of danger)

In every case, walking through these doorways of fear has led to a greater experience of God's presence and power in my life. And even on those occasions when I've walked through one of these doorways, and things didn't go the way I hoped, I still experienced God's sufficiency in a personal way, as I discovered that He really can sustain me through whatever He calls me to.

So what doorway of fear is God calling you to walk through so that He can reveal to you that He's bigger than any fear that may have its grip on you?

JESUS' WORD TO THE CHURCH AT SMYRNA: COURAGE

Responding to Jesus' Letter

1) Name that fear or specific assignment you sense God calling you to. Write it down on the doorway below, and then prayerfully visualize yourself walking through that doorway with God's help.

2) Then pray this prayer:

   Lord Jesus, I pray that You would either release me from my feelings of fear, or give me a Spirit-inspired courage to face this fear. Even if I still feel afraid in this area of my life, may I no longer be paralyzed by it. To drive this truth home to my heart, I invite You to give me an opportunity to face this fear, and to do what You're calling me to – so that I can meet You in a profound way, and discover that You really are bigger than my fear.

Digging Deeper

1) Do an internet search of 'Francis Chan Balance Beam' and watch a powerful 3-minute illustration of why we don't want to live in bondage to our fears.

2) Put the song, *In Christ Alone,* on your playlist, and listen to it when you need a reminder that there is no place for paralyzing fear for those who belong to Jesus.

3) Read *Insanity of God* (by Nik Ripken), and be inspired and challenged by the bold, courageous faith of our persecuted brothers and sisters in Christ from around the world.

4

JESUS' WORD TO THE CHURCH AT PERGAMUM: PURITY

GROWING UP, I LOVED BOARD GAMES. SO much so that my little sister was frequently the victim of me harassing her to play. I could usually convince her to start the game, but about fifteen minutes in, she would typically announce, "I don't want to play anymore."

Since I was neurotically competitive, I wouldn't let her off the hook that easily. "You agreed to play," I would say. To which she would respond, "I *did* play, I just don't want to play *anymore*." At which point I would play the morality card, accusing her of lying. "I didn't lie," she would say, "I just changed my mind." I would then use every manipulative tactic in the book to try to make her keep playing, until at some point she would throw down the ultimate trump card, declaring, "You can't make me play… because *you're not the boss of me!*" And even though I really wanted to be the boss of her, I knew she was right. I was not the boss of her.

Game over. Literally.

It's empowering to tell someone who is trying to lord it over us that they're not our boss. But let me ask: if you're a Christian, who *is* the boss of you? And I don't mean who is your employer. I mean who is the one who tells you what you can or can't do *in every area of life?*

Who is the boss of you?

Contrary to what many of us think, I am not the boss of me. I am not the captain of my own ship. I am not the master of my own destiny. Yes, there is freedom for those who belong to Jesus, but we're not free to do whatever we want (Galatians 5:13).

Translation: I'm not the boss of me.

When I put my trust in Jesus, it's not just that I got my sins forgiven so I can go to heaven when I die. My life was ransomed, *purchased* by the blood of Jesus. Redemption, by definition, means that I am no longer my own. The legal title of my mind, soul, and body has been transferred into Jesus' name. He is my Master now. I belong to Him (1 Corinthians 6:19-20).

Purity is living in the reality that I *belong* to Jesus; that He is the One to whom I now gladly submit. Unfortunately, even though I know Jesus is the One who is to be calling the shots in my life, my tendency, at times, is to slip into auto-pilot, and live like I'm in charge. That's what happened to the church at Pergamum, too. The believers were living as if they were their own boss. False teachers had infiltrated them, promoting the lie that as long as they believed in Jesus they were free to do whatever they wanted. Essentially, God's grace became a license to sin.

This phenomenon is growing more prevalent in the church in America today, too. Purity is no longer viewed as our appropriate response to God's grace. Instead it's often portrayed as prudish, legalistic, an obstacle to our enjoyment of life. But Jesus hasn't changed His mind about purity. When He returns for us, He wants a Bride who is *pure*, "dressed in white linen, which stand for the righteous acts of the saints" (Rev 20:8). PURITY isn't just Jesus' word to the ancient church at Pergamum. It's also His word for us today.

> "To the angel of the church in Pergamum write: These are the words of him who has the sharp, double-edged sword. I know where you live— where Satan has his throne. Yet you remain true to my name. You did not renounce your

faith in me, not even in the days of Antipas, my faithful witness, who was put to death in your city—where Satan lives.

Nevertheless, I have a few things against you: There are some among you who hold to the teaching of Balaam, who taught Balak to entice the Israelites to sin so that they ate food sacrificed to idols and committed sexual immorality. Likewise, you also have those who hold to the teaching of the Nicolaitans. Repent therefore! Otherwise, I will soon come to you and will fight against them with the sword of my mouth.

Whoever has ears, let them hear what the Spirit says to the churches. To the one who is victorious, I will give some of the hidden manna. I will also give that person a white stone with a new name written on it, known only to the one who receives it."
~ Revelation 2:12-17

Historical Context: The Significance of the Sword

Jesus introduced himself in this letter very intentionally as the one "who has the sharp, double-edged sword" (v12). He knew it would grab their attention because the governor of Pergamum had just been given "the right to bear the sword" ('Ius Gladii') by Caesar. 'Gladii' is the Greek word from which we get our English word, 'gladiator.' 'Ius Gladii' was the term used to describe 'the right to execute criminals.' The right to execute was reserved for Caesar, but had recently been bestowed upon the governor of Pergamum for becoming the first city in the province of Asia to build a temple in honor of the emperor. As a reward for kissing up to his boss, the governor was given, 'Ius Gladii.'

The sword had huge significance in Pergamum. It was the icon of their city, the symbol the governor used to boast of how he held the power over life and death, just like Caesar. Jesus, then, the Master-Communicator, aware of Pergamum's pride on this subject, introduces *Himself* as the One with "the sharp, double-edged sword" – to remind His people who is actually in charge. He is the One with the sword, the One who determines life or death. Not the governor. Not Caesar.

Jesus' sword, though, is not a typical sword. It's not the sword of a gladiator. The sword isn't even in his *hand*. According to the opening chapter of Revelation, the sword is in Jesus' *mouth*: "and out of his mouth came a double-edged sword" (Rev 1:16). The sword is the Word of God. As Hebrews 4:12 says: "For the Word of God is… sharper than any double-edged sword." In other words, when Jesus speaks, people are cut to the heart with God's truth. Jesus is the One who has the sword. Therefore, He is the One with the authority, and the One we are to listen to.

In Praise of Pergamum

As is Jesus' custom, whenever there is anything in the church to commend, He is generous with praise. And there is much in the church at Pergamum to commend. Jesus says they "remained true to His name" and "refused to renounce their faith" (v13), even when it cost them their lives.

The city of Pergamum was so antagonistic against Christianity that Jesus said it was where Satan "lives and has his throne" (v13). Not that Satan had a literal throne in Pergamum. Jesus was referring to the Imperial Cult. Pergamum was the official center for emperor worship in the province of Asia, which meant extreme persecution for His followers.

Nevertheless, the believers in Pergamum refused to renounce their faith. Antipas, their pastor, became the first martyr in the province of Asia. According to church history, Antipas was slow-roasted to death in a bronze kettle for refusing to deny his faith in Christ. Many other members of the church followed his example, for which Jesus praises them:

> "I know where you live—where Satan has his throne. Yet you remain true to my name. You did not renounce your faith in me, not even in the days of Antipas, my faithful witness, who was put to death in your city—where Satan lives."
> ~ Revelation 2:13

Despite living on the frontlines of the battle against Satan and the Imperial Cult, they refused to renounce their faith in Jesus, even when *the sword* was literally at their neck. And for that, Jesus commends them.

Satan Trades in the Sword for Seduction

But Satan rarely settles for using the same weapon if it's not working. He's crafty, and has many weapons in his arsenal. Since the *sword* wasn't working to get the believers to deny their faith, Satan switched to using *seduction*. He infiltrated the church through the Nicolaitans, the same false teachers who tried to take over the church at Ephesus. The Nicolaitans taught that as long as you didn't outright renounce your faith in Jesus, you were free to indulge in any number of sinful pleasures. The church at Ephesus threw out these false teachers. But the church at Pergamum bought into their lies. This is where Jesus' commendation ends, and his correction begins.

> "Nevertheless, I have a few things against you: There are some among you who hold to the teaching of Balaam, who taught Balak to entice the Israelites to sin so that they ate food sacrificed to idols and

> committed sexual immorality. Likewise, you also have those who hold to the teaching of the Nicolaitans."
>
> ~ Revelation 2:14-15

The Nicolaitans were the "spiritual grandparents" of those who, today, teach that as long we believe in Jesus, we can live however we want to. They were religious, and spoke in spiritual terms. But they promoted moral compromise, seducing God's people into eating food sacrificed to idols and to committing sexual immorality. In doing so, they were destroying the church from within. As Darrell Johnson says, "While the Christians of Pergamum were resisting the influence from without, they were carelessly indifferent to the influence from within... Although the church was being vigilant on the front lines it was tolerating a Trojan horse in its midst."[20]

Overt persecution had failed to take out the church in Pergamum. Even killing their pastor didn't work. And so, instead of continuing to use the *sword* against them, Satan's next tactic was to weaken them through *seduction*, "enticing" them to follow the teaching of Balaam (Rev 3:14).

According to Numbers 25 and 31, Balaam was a sorcerer, who had been hired by an enemy of Israel to put a curse on them. But every time Balaam opened his mouth to curse Israel, blessings poured out instead. Trying to take down God's people from the outside failed. So you know what they say: *if you can't beat 'em, join 'em*. That's what Balaam did. He joined Israel. And over time, that's how he sabotaged their walk with God. Not with curses, but with compromise. Not with a sword, but with seduction. Not with a weapon from the outside, but with a weapon on the inside. Balaam slithered into Israel's camp, masqueraded as one of them, learned their spiritual lingo, and over time, seduced them into idolatry and sexual immorality.

This is what happened in Pergamum, too, which is why Jesus calls their false teachers: Balaam.

JESUS' WORD TO THE CHURCH AT PERGAMUM: PURITY

Was there actually a teacher named Balaam in the church at Pergamum? Not likely. Jesus is saying that these false teachers were cut from the same religious cloth as Balaam. They were to the church in Pergamum what Balaam was to Israel. And Satan was the one behind their sabotage, luring the church into believing that sexual immorality and eating food sacrificed to idols was okay.

Historical Context of Food Sacrificed to Idols

Sexual immorality is certainly more of an issue in our culture than eating food sacrificed to idols. The temptation of sexual sin is as real today in our culture as at any point in human history. That's why, when we look at the letter Jesus sent to the church at Thyatira (another church being seduced into sexual sin), we'll focus in on that subject. But eating food sacrificed to idols was a significant issue, too. And once we understand why, we'll see how Jesus' words still apply to us.

My guess is that eating food sacrificed to idols is not a big temptation for most of us. But what if our livelihood was dependent upon it? That was the situation for the working class people in Pergamum. If you wanted to do business in Pergamum, you needed to attend the trade guild meetings. And attending these meetings meant participating in a meal where you worshiped that trade guild's god – *by eating food sacrificed to that particular idol.* You could refuse, but not without being kicked out of the trade guild. And that meant being cut off from the social network that could help you maintain your business. Abstaining from the trade guild was financial suicide.

Christians who abstained had to face the question: "How will I feed my family if I don't join the trade guild?" Refusing to eat the food sacrificed to idols called for a radical trust in God's provision, which is exactly what Jesus promises at the end of His letter:

> "To the one who is victorious, I will give some of the hidden manna…"
>
> ~ Revelation 2:17

Manna was the daily food from heaven that God provided His people when they were wandering through the wilderness for forty years. Here, "manna" is the provision that God promises His people in Pergamum, *if they will stay true to Him and trust Him to provide.* In other words, instead of the short-term financial security that could be theirs if they joined the trade guilds, Jesus offers supernatural provision from heaven.

That's the kind of promise Jesus is making to His people in Pergamum (and to us) – *if* we pursue purity and refuse to compromise. Of course, refusing to compromise is easier said than done – especially when life gets tough, or when finances get tight, or when our dreams aren't panning out. Isn't that when we're most susceptible to temptation? Isn't that when we're most inclined to get seduced by that thing we know isn't good – because we think it'll make us feel better – at least momentarily? Isn't that when we start to hear Satan whispering in our ear, *Oh, your life is so hard. You deserve it. Just do it. It's not like you're renouncing your faith.*

For most of us, Satan using the sword to try to make us deny Jesus is too obvious a ploy. Sure, it would be scary to have someone threaten to kill us if we refused to renounce our faith. But we'd see the threat for what it is. Seduction, though subtle, is often more effective. It might take a while to do its thing, but over time, it still takes us out, like the proverbial frog in the boiling pot.

Pergamum in Us

So let me ask: Is there an area in your life where you're compromising and rationalizing it:

- Watching stuff that dishonors God, and rationalizing: "Well, everyone's watching it"
- Abusing alcohol/prescription drugs, and rationalizing: "I just need to take the edge off"
- Not gathering together with the church as God's Word clearly calls us to do, and rationalizing: "I just have a lot of other things going on right now"

- Wasting hours on social media, and rationalizing: "I'm keeping up with my friends"
- Eating in secret, compulsive ways and rationalizing: "I'm not doing drugs; it's just food"
- Gossiping, and rationalizing: "I'm just making sure people know the real story"
- Not sharing the gospel, and rationalizing: "Evangelism just isn't my gift"
- Not giving, and rationalizing: "I'm just in a tight season financially"
- Shading the truth, and rationalizing: "It's not like I'm outright lying"
- Going into debt to buy stuff, and rationalizing: "It was just too good a deal to pass up"
- Not reading the Bible, and rationalizing: "It's just too hard to understand"
- Looking at porn, and rationalizing: "It's only affecting me; it's not hurting anybody else"
- Neglecting family, and rationalizing: "I've just got a lot on my plate right now"
- Flirting with someone who is married, and rationalizing: "I'm just being friendly"
- Shrinking back from that serving opportunity God keeps calling me to, and rationalizing: "I just don't think I have it in me to serve God in that way"
- Losing your temper and yelling/cursing, and rationalizing: "I just can't help it"
- Being passive about discipling your kids, and rationalizing: "I just don't know how"
- Holding onto that addiction, and rationalizing: "I've tried to quit, but I just can't live without it"

The point of an inventory exercise like this one is to help us get honest about those places in life where we're compromising – so that we can bring them to the cross and repent of them. The cross isn't just for those who first realize they need a Savior. It's also for long-time Christians, who have allowed 'compromise' to sabotage their walk with their Savior. For both, the answer is the cross.

So once you've identified a place in your life where you're compromising and rationalizing:

1) <u>Run to the Cross</u>: confessing it, and acknowledging your ongoing need for a Savior.

2) <u>Renounce your sin at the Cross</u>: committing yourself to get serious about it, sharing it with a trusted friend, pastor or counselor, who can pray for you, encourage you, and help you get at the root of why this sin is seducing you.

3) <u>Rejoice in the Cross</u>: basking in the assurance that, because of Jesus' finished work, you can stand before God pure, without any shame or condemnation.

Take a few minutes to do that right now. Write down on the cross the word that represents that place in your life where you've allowed compromise into your walk with God. Maybe it's: "work" or "entertainment" or "alcohol" or "pornography" or "food" or "finances" or "marriage" or "dating relationship." Maybe it's something else. Then, after renouncing it and rejoicing that God has made you pure through the finished work of Christ, ask Him to help you walk in purity in this area of life. Jesus is coming back for His Bride, and He wants us not just to be *declared* pure, but to *walk* in purity – which is what the second part of this chapter is all about.

JESUS' WORD TO THE CHURCH AT PERGAMUM: PURITY

"If we confess our sins, he is faithful and just and will forgive us our sins and purify us from all unrighteousness" (1 John 1:9).

Walking in Purity

At the cross, God did *for* us everything we need to be declared pure. But He also wants to do something *in* us – so we can walk in purity. The question is: 'Do we want that?' For some of us, our desire for purity is like that of Saint Augustine, who shortly after coming to faith in Jesus, prayed, "Lord, I want to be pure… but not yet."

Even if we do *want* to live a life of purity, though, our will power is not enough to get us there. In our own strength, our resolve eventually weakens. And then, in a moment of temptation, we slip up, compromise, and settle for something we think will bring us a little happiness. After we give in, though, we feel discouraged, guilty and ashamed. Then we promise God we'll do better next time. But before long, we find ourselves falling right back into it again, giving in to that same temptation.

We've received *forgiveness for* that sin, but we don't yet have *freedom from* that sin.

Is that just our lot in life? Are we destined to live a life of powerlessness over sin? No! Jesus came to bring us forgiveness *and* freedom. That's what the rest of Jesus' letter to the church at

Pergamum is all about: showing us the way to live out the purity He won for us at the cross.

The Way to Purity = Repentance

Jesus only has *one* word of instruction in this letter: "Repent!"

> "Repent therefore! Otherwise, I will soon come to you and will fight against them with the sword of my mouth."
> ~ Revelation 2:16

Repentance is the key to walking in purity. Unfortunately, *repentance* has become one of those religious words that's often misunderstood in our culture. Literally, *to repent* means "to change one's mind." That's why Jesus tells His people that if they don't repent, He will come and fight against "them" (the Nicolaitans) with "the sword of His mouth" (His Word). Jesus is saying He is going to come and do battle against the false teachers with the truth of His Word. As Jesus says in John 8:32, if His people know the truth, "the truth will set them free." So the fight against temptation and compromise begin, not in our wills, but in our minds. Jesus knows if He can win the battle for our minds, purity will follow. That's why His only command to this church is to repent, to "change their minds."

Repentance = A Crisis Decision Followed by a Process

One aspect of repentance happens in an instant, when our mind is opened to the truth of the gospel, we realize our rebellion against God, we see our need for a Savior, and we turn to Him and say, *"Lord, I acknowledge I'm a sinner. I want to turn away from my sin and turn to You as the Savior and Lord of my life. Thank You for Your work on the cross that purchased my forgiveness. Help me to no longer live for myself, but for You."*

However, if you're anything like me, just because you prayed a prayer of repentance once, doesn't mean you won't ever struggle with sin. That's because there is another dimension of repentance besides the crisis decision. Repentance is also a process. Changing the way we think doesn't happen overnight. It happens on a daily basis, little by little, as we learn what it means to have the mind of Christ in every area of our lives (1 Corinthians 2:16). When we become a Christian, the Spirit doesn't zap us, and instantaneously set us free from wrong patterns of thinking and every inclination to sin. Yes, He indwells us, and He gives us a new power over sin that we've never had before. But He also conforms us into the image of Jesus *over time*, as we learn to surrender our minds and every aspect of our lives to Him.

Crisis + Process.

Disclaimer: God *can* instantaneously deliver us from certain sins the moment we repent and come to faith in Christ. But often, there are old habits and old ways of thinking that God transforms over time. In the Old Testament, God got Israel out of Egypt in one day. But it took forty years to get Egypt out of Israel. The analogy breaks down, but there's a parallel in the New Testament. Jesus frees us from the penalty of sin in a moment. And because His Spirit now dwells within us (from that moment on) we're no longer slaves to sin. But learning to walk in the power of the Spirit is a process, one that doesn't always happen overnight. If it did, we wouldn't have most of the New Testament, which is made up of letters, written to *Christians*, helping them know how to live out what Jesus did for them at the cross!

Learning to walk in purity is a transformational process that is kick-started by the renewing of our minds. This is why Paul, in Romans 12:2, says: "Do not conform any longer to the pattern of this world, but be transformed by the renewing of your mind." The battle against compromise begins between our ears, whether the temptation is gossip, gluttony, greed, anger, anxiety, pornography, or any other sin. And God doesn't give our brains a lobotomy to eliminate every old pattern of thinking. He calls *us* to renew our minds. And that takes time and intentionality.

Randy Alcorn, author of *The Purity Principle*, describes the process:

> The kind of person we are becoming is determined by what we are taking into our brains... The old saying is true: 'Sow a thought, reap an action; sow an action, reap a habit; sow a habit, reap a character; sow a character, reap a destiny.' Actions, habits, character, and destiny *all start with a thought*...21

Don't Think about Snakes

All moral compromise begins with a thought. Sin is always birthed the same way: we think about something we shouldn't be thinking about, and then, eventually, we act on that thought:

- Before we go to that website, we're *thinking* about that website.
- Before we blow our paycheck at the casino, we're *thinking* about that casino.
- Before we eat that whole cake, we're *thinking* about that cake.

The way to victory over sin is to "repent", to change the way we *think*. Of course, it's not as simple as telling yourself to *stop* thinking those thoughts that lead to compromise. After all, have you ever tried really hard to *make* yourself stop thinking about something? Listen to Randy Alcorn explain why this doesn't work, and how there's a better way:

> Just for a moment, I'd like you to follow my instruction. Ready? Don't think about snakes. I repeat, *do not* think about big, slimy snakes, coming up from your bathtub drain at night and slithering into your bed. You heard me. *Don't*

think about snakes. Have I kept you from thinking about snakes? No. I've *encouraged* you to think about them.

Now, I want you to envision your favorite dessert. Perhaps it's your mother's Dutch apple pie, or chocolate chip cookies, or Jamoca Almond Fudge ice cream, or a Butterfinger Blizzard. Just think about that mouth-watering treat.

What happened in the last few moments? You'd forgotten all about the slithering snakes, hadn't you…until I just mentioned them again.

Our minds are not vacuums. They will be filled with *something*. Impure thoughts are pushed out by pure thoughts, which is why the Apostle Paul says: 'Whatever is true, whatever is noble, whatever is right, whatever is pure, think about such things.'[22]

The way to deal with thoughts that tempt us to compromise is not by telling ourselves to stop thinking those thoughts, but to *replace* them with thoughts that are true, good, and pure.

Spiritual Practices to Combat Compromise

I've certainly not arrived when it comes to experiencing full and final victory over compromise and temptation. But Jesus is helping me – through several practices that are empowering me to grow in that direction. These are exercises to turn to when you find yourself listening to the seductive voice of the enemy: thinking about that person you know you're not supposed to be with, thinking about secretly gorging yourself on that dessert, thinking about clicking on that website you know you shouldn't go to, thinking about buying that thing you don't need, or doing that thing you know you'll regret doing.

1) Honest Prayer

One of the most important things I've learned to do when compromising thoughts enter my mind is to get honest with God about them. I don't beat myself up about them. I don't pretend they're not there. I don't try really hard to get them out of my head. But neither do I rationalize them. I confess them. I own my sin. I call a spade a spade. And as I do so, Satan's power over me is diminished. That's what happens whenever I tell the truth and bring temptation into the light of the Lord's presence. I then ask God to help me replace these tempting thoughts with thoughts of His goodness and His love, and especially what He did for me at Calvary, which leads me to...

2) Turn to the Cross

After honest prayer, I turn my mental gaze to the cross. I reflect on what Christ did for me there, and how He took upon Himself all of my sins. This practice is a way to lean into the truth that the cross isn't just the means of God *forgiving* me the *punishment* of my sin; it's also the means of God *freeing* me from the *power* of my sin. More and more these days, I'm realizing that victory over sin doesn't happen from me trying harder not to sin. It happens as I dwell deeply on the reality of what Christ has already done to defeat sin.

3) Accountability

One of the most important things I need to do, if I want to live a life of purity, is to regularly meet and pray with trusted friends. People who love Jesus. People who want to see me grow. People who know the places in my life where I have a tendency to compromise. People who know the questions I need to be asked. People I can call or send a text to when I'm feeling tempted or discouraged. People who can encourage me, pray for me, and challenge me. People who invite me to do the same for them.

Satan loves it when we try to face temptation all on our own. Lone ranger spirituality is a trap. Don't fall for it. Satan will pick you off if you do. He prowls around (1 Peter 5:8), looking to devour the straggler, who's trying to fight sin on their own. But there is power that comes when we share our temptations with others. Find an accountability partner or a small group where you can get honest and find encouragement for those areas of your life where you're tempted. If you don't find a group like this right away, ask your pastor to help you find one. Keep praying and looking for one until you do.

4) Memorizing Strategic Scriptures

This might be the most important way I've learned to arrest compromising thoughts. Here's how it works: let's say pornography is an area where you're tempted to compromise. In addition to joining a group where you can get honest and find encouragement in your struggle (and be reminded of the truth of the gospel), memorize a verse like Job 31:1, which says, "I have made a covenant with my eyes to not look lustfully at a girl."

Then spend time every morning for a few weeks reciting this verse to yourself – so that, later in the day, if you're tempted to look at something you shouldn't look at – your mind is triggered to go back to this Scripture. Don't just tell yourself: 'Stop thinking about porn.' Preach God's Word to yourself. Memorizing Scripture is not the silver bullet, but there is power in declaring God's Word to yourself and Satan. It's the strategy Jesus employed when He was tempted to compromise (Matthew 4:4, 7, 10). We would do well to follow His example.

Perhaps food is an area where you're tempted to compromise. I'm having lots of conversations with people these days who sense the Spirit's conviction on this subject. Not just: "I need to lose weight," but "Food is a stronghold in my life." If that's you, then in addition to joining a group that can support you in this journey, memorize a verse like Deut 8:3, which says: "Man shall not live by bread alone, but by every word that comes from the mouth of the Lord." Put that verse on your refrigerator door or on your kitchen cupboard as a way of redirecting your thoughts.

Perhaps money is an area where you're tempted to compromise. Maybe you're tempted to spend it in ways that you know you shouldn't, because you slip into thinking that the money in your wallet or savings account is actually *your* money. If that's you, then you might want to consider memorizing a verse like Psalm 24:1, which says: "The earth is the Lord's, and everything in it." Put that verse inside your wallet or purse, or next to where you keep your credit cards, or as the screen saver for your computer, if that's how you buy things or pay the bills.

Perhaps people-pleasing is an area in your life where you struggle. Maybe you're tempted to think more about what other people think of you than what God thinks of you. If that's you, you might want to memorize a verse like Galatians 1:10, where Paul says, "Am I trying to win the approval of men or of God? Or am I trying to please men? If I was still trying to please men, I wouldn't be a servant of Christ." Put that verse on your bathroom mirror, so that every morning, before you go to work, school or church, you're reminded of whose opinion of you really matters. Recite it to yourself whenever you find yourself dwelling too much on what 'so and so' thinks of you.

Whether you're tempted to compromise in the area of sexuality, money, food, people-pleasing, whatever – the victory over sin begins in our minds. "Be transformed," Paul says, "by the renewing of your minds" (Romans 12:2).

Honest prayer. Turning your gaze to the cross. Accountability. Memorizing Strategic Scripture. These spiritual practices have tremendous power in training us to walk in purity.

Promise of a White Stone

Like all seven of Jesus' letters, this one to the church at Pergamum concludes with a promise that is tailor made for them:

> "To the one who overcomes, I will give a white stone with a new name written on it, known only to the one who receives it."
> ~ Revelation 2:17

JESUS' WORD TO THE CHURCH AT PERGAMUM: PURITY

White stones were used in the Roman Empire as admission tokens to pagan festivals, the kind of drunken love feasts that Christians, who wanted to remain pure, did not attend. Jesus promises His followers in Pergamum a *white stone* to remind them that they have something far better to look forward to than any party this world is throwing. A white stone is Jesus' ways of telling them, *You may feel like you're missing out on some of the pleasures and provisions of this world, but stay pure. Don't give in. Don't compromise. The party I'm preparing for you is literally out of this world!*

There's something else Jesus probably had in mind when He promised a white stone. In ancient Roman execution court trials, juries used a black stone to vote 'guilty', and a white stone to vote 'not guilty.' Before being executed, it is likely that Pastor Antipas would have been given a black stone for refusing to worship Caesar as Lord. The promise of a white stone is a reminder that if we've been washed in the purifying blood of Christ, then no matter what anyone else might say about us, or what verdict the world gives us, Jesus himself will enter that eternal courtroom and overrule every black stone that's ever been handed to us. Instead, He will give each of us a white stone that pronounces: "Not guilty! No more condemnation for those who are in Christ Jesus!" (Romans 8:1).

And then from that courtroom, Jesus will whisk us away to that eternal wedding banquet. And because we've got that white stone in our hand (the admission ticket, if you will) – we'll hear a voice from inside the door of the party beckoning to us, "Come on in. The feast of all feasts, the celebration of all celebrations, the party of all parties, is just getting started!"

So whenever you're tempted to compromise, settling for short-term pleasures, remember there's a feast coming that will make every alluring sin this world has to offer look like chopped liver. There's an eternal celebration coming that will be so great, it will make you wonder why you were ever tempted by lesser things. There's a party in Heaven that will be well worth the wait!

Responding to Jesus' Letter

Identify one area in your life (even if there are several) where you are tempted to compromise, and then develop a training regimen for arresting those thoughts before they lead to sin.

1) <u>Honest Prayer</u>. Every time you feel tempted to compromise, stop and take that thought to God in an honest prayer. Don't beat yourself up over it. Don't try to *make* yourself stop thinking it. Just acknowledge honestly to God that it's there, and then ask Him to help you replace that tempting thought with thoughts of His goodness, His love, and the cross. Don't be discouraged if you find yourself doing this multiple times throughout the day.

2) <u>Turn your gaze to the cross</u>. Personally, I sometimes carry a nail around in my pocket to help me go there. However you do it, intentionally turn your focus to the cross, reflecting on the truth of what Jesus did to *forgive* you and *free* you from sin.

3) <u>Accountability</u>. Begin praying for and seeking out a small group where you can get honest with others about this area in life where you're compromising. Talk to your pastor about finding such a group. If there isn't a small group for you to join, pray about starting one. I guarantee that you are not the only one in your church who would benefit from such a group.

4) <u>Memorize Strategic Scriptures</u>. Find a simple, easy-to-memorize verse that you can recite in those moments when you sense yourself becoming vulnerable to temptation. If you need help finding a relevant Scripture that speaks to the specific area in life where you're tempted – simply type into an internet search engine, "Bible verses to help with _____."

JESUS' WORD TO THE CHURCH AT PERGAMUM: PURITY

Digging Deeper

1) Listen to *Jesus Paid it All*, and be reminded and encouraged by the good news of what Christ did to purify you of sin.

2) Read *The Purity Principle* (by Randy Alcorn), which not only makes a great case for the importance of purity, but also charts a course for how to walk in purity.

3) Read *All In* (by Mark Batterson), a book filled with inspiring stories of how a life fully devoted to Jesus is not only more fulfilling, but will be used by God to impact the world.

4) Consider utilizing these resources for your entertainment and technology worlds:

- www.pluggedin.com – a great resource for previewing movies and other media in order to help you and your family walk in purity in your entertainment world.
- www.clearplay.com & www.vidangel.com – filtering systems that allow you to watch movies without the gratuitous violence, sex, and profanity.
- www.covenanteyes.com – an internet accountability system that gives a report of what you've viewed (on your computer, tablet, phone, etc.) to an accountability partner.

5

JESUS' WORD TO THE CHURCH AT THYATIRA: REPENTANCE

ONE OF THE HARDEST THINGS I'VE EVER had to do was confront a good friend who was romantically involved with someone who didn't follow Jesus. As a believer, he knew he wasn't supposed to be with this person (1 Cor 6-7), but he rationalized it as no big deal. And sadly, none of his Christian friends called him out on it, me included. I shared my concerns with him in a round-about sort of way. In other words, I pulled punches. I chickened out. I failed to call him out. And I rationalized that my failure to confront him was born out of love for him. But eventually, the Lord convicted me of my cowardice, and gave me a picture of what I was actually doing to my friend: *passively standing by, as he walked toward a cliff.*

Finally, I stopped mincing my words, and said what I should have said earlier: to stop playing games with God, repent, turn back to Jesus, and break up with this woman. When he laughed me off as being overly dramatic, I told him I was going to pray that his eyes be opened to the gravity of his sin, and how he was grieving Jesus. I said it as graciously as I could, but also with a sense of urgency. I knew that he knew I loved him. Still, he dismissed me, saying I was making a mountain out of a molehill. That's how the conversation ended.

A few days later, he called me, shaken up, struggling to describe what had happened to him that morning. He said he awoke so burdened by the weight of his sin that he started weeping. (I've rarely seen this friend cry or get emotional.) He said he could so clearly *feel* his sin that he couldn't stop crying. He confessed and repented before he even got out of bed. Later that same day he broke off the relationship. That was over twenty years ago. Today he is married to a woman who loves God, their children are all following Christ, and he is still a good friend.

I wish all confrontation stories had that kind of happy ending. But they don't – which is why many of us shy away from confrontation. It doesn't always go well. It's not easy to tell people the truth when we know it might hurt or offend. I know I don't always enjoy it when people call me out. It kicks against my pride. I get defensive. My flesh doesn't want to hear it – especially if I sense the person who is calling me out doesn't really care about me. On the other hand, if I know the person calling me out loves me, I might resist at first (because, by nature, I am a defensive person), but I eventually listen, because I know they're just trying to keep me from walking off a spiritual cliff.

That's what we need to remember when Jesus calls us out. He's doing it because *He loves us enough to warn us when we're about to walk off a cliff.* That's the heart behind Jesus' letter to the church at Thyatira. The believers were buying into the lie that they could worship God and freely live in sexual sin, without needing to repent. The point of His letter was not to condemn them, but to wake them up, and to help them understand the severity of their situation. That's what Jesus is reaching for whenever His people are playing around in sin and rationalizing it as no big deal: repentance. That's why "REPENT" isn't just an apt word for the church in Thyatira. It's a fitting word for any of us who are walking toward a spiritual cliff.

> "To the angel of the church in Thyatira write:
> These are the words of the Son of God,
> whose eyes are like blazing fire and whose

JESUS' WORD TO THE CHURCH AT THYATIRA: REPENTANCE

feet are like burnished bronze. I know your deeds, your love and faith, your service and perseverance, and that you are now doing more than you did at first.

Nevertheless, I have this against you: You tolerate that woman Jezebel, who calls herself a prophet. By her teaching she misleads my servants into sexual immorality and the eating of food sacrificed to idols. I have given her time to repent of her immorality, but she is unwilling to repent. So I will cast her on a bed of suffering, and I will make those who commit adultery with her suffer intensely, unless they repent of her ways. I will strike her children dead. Then all the churches will know that I am he who searches hearts and minds, and I will repay each of you according to your deeds.

Now I say to the rest of you in Thyatira, to you who do not hold to her teaching and have not learned Satan's so-called deep secrets, 'I will not impose any other burden on you, except to hold on to what you have until I come.'

To the one who is victorious and does my will to the end, I will give authority over the nations— that one 'will rule them with an iron scepter and will dash them to pieces like pottery' — just as I have received authority from my Father. I will also give that one the morning star. Whoever has ears, let them hear what the Spirit says to the churches."
~ Revelation 2:18-29

Historical Background

The city of Thyatira was dedicated to the worship of Apollo. He was the god being honored at all of their trade guild meetings, the one to whom every citizen of the city gave their allegiance. In Greek mythology, Apollo was the son of the high god, Zeus. It's not a coincidence that Jesus introduces himself in this letter as "the Son of God" (v18). It was a jab at Apollo, Jesus' way of saying, "Apollo is not the Son of God. I Am." The implication, of course, is that *Jesus* is the One we are to listen to, not Apollo, and certainly not this false prophet, "Jezebel" (v20), who was teaching it was okay to worship God *and* indulge in sexual sin.

Jezebel was most likely not her real name. It was a moniker Jesus gave this false teacher to wake up His people to who had infiltrated their church. We do a similar thing today when we call someone "Judas" or "Benedict Arnold." We're not calling them by their actual name. We're calling out their behavior, their offense. That's what Jesus is doing here.

To understand exactly what Jesus is calling out in this false prophet, we need to know something about the historical Jezebel. Queen Jezebel came into power in Israel through her marriage to King Ahab. The daughter of the King of Tyre, Jezebel was infamous for promoting the worship of the false god, Baal. What's interesting, though, is that (at least at the beginning of her reign) she didn't try to snuff out everything to do with the Lord. She had a more covert game plan. Darrell Johnson describes her strategy:

> Jezebel's public argument was that one could worship Baal right alongside Yahweh. But she knew better. She knew that different religious systems, at least those so fundamentally different as Baal worship and Yahweh worship, cannot exist side-by-side without compromising one or both. And she knew the clear teaching of Israel's prophets: that when it came to worshiping Yahweh it is 'either/or' not 'both/and.' 'You shall have no other gods

> before me,' says Yahweh (Exodus 20:3). Any kind of compromise is out of the question. The choice is 'Yahweh *or* Baal,' not 'Yahweh *and* Baal.'23

Jezebel's strategy was to promote "Yahweh *and* Baal," knowing that this would eventually lead to the end of true worship of God in Israel. It was a long-con plan. Most people think Jezebel wanted to immediately eliminate everything associated with the Lord, but that's not accurate, at least not at the beginning of her reign. In fact, Jezebel and Ahab even named one of their sons, Joram, in honor of God. Joram means: *The Lord is exalted.*

Jezebel wasn't opposed to worshiping God; she was opposed to *only* worshiping God. She was tolerant of God being worshiped – as long as it didn't get in the way of Baal being worshipped. This is what's called religious syncretism, the attempt to combine two very different belief systems. Syncretism is the religion that Ahab and Jezebel promoted. It's why, when Elijah preached to Ahab and the people of Israel on Mount Carmel, his message to them was:

> "How long will you waver (literally "dance") between two opinions? If the Lord is God, follow Him. If Baal is God, follow him"(1 Kings 18:21).

Elijah's preaching ministry was about confronting the religious syncretism of Israel.

Jesus was confronting the same thing in the church at Thyatira.

Religious Syncretism Today

Syncretism isn't just an ancient phenomenon. It's alive today all over the world. I recently read an article about the religious syncretism of Haiti. The author described how Haiti is 70% Catholic, 30% Protestant, and 90% Voodoo. Do the math. Those numbers don't work, unless there is some serious syncretism going on, some "both/and" at play.

Leslie Griffiths, an expert on Haiti, and a supporter of the decision to list Voodoo alongside Catholicism as its national religion, said: "It's not unusual for Haitians to be both in the world of voodoo and in the world of Roman Catholicism." When asked: "Why practice Voodoo *and* Roman Catholicism?" Griffiths said: "95% of voodoo is simply the invoking of spirits to help people survive what is sometimes a very difficult life."[24] In other words, Christianity might be what most people in Haiti say they believe, but voodoo is what many turn to when they're not sure if God will be enough to satisfy their longings or heal their hurts.

I don't want to pick on Haiti, though. We American believers have our own versions of syncretism, things we turn to in order to satisfy our longings or deal with disappointment. Many of us worship Jesus on Sunday and then give ourselves to false gods during the week, chasing after whatever we think will make us happy: pleasure, success, toys, comfort, and the approval of others. Christianity might be our official religion, but if Jesus doesn't come through for us in the ways we want Him to, we've got our back-up gods we turn to in order to get us through.

That's what was happening in Thyatira. The church was following Jesus *and* indulging in sexual sin and idolatry that "Jezebel" taught was okay. And there's no way to sugar coat what Jesus says about this syncretism. He issues the strongest warning possible:

> "You tolerate that woman Jezebel, who calls herself a prophet. By her teaching she misleads my servants into sexual immorality and the eating of food sacrificed to idols. I have given her time to repent of her immorality, but she is unwilling. So I will cast her on a bed of suffering, and I will make those who commit adultery with her suffer intensely, unless they repent of her ways. I will strike her children dead."
> ~ Revelation 2:20-23

JESUS' WORD TO THE CHURCH AT THYATIRA: REPENTANCE

Tough words to hear. But Jesus said them. So we need to take them seriously.

Disclaimer: when Jesus talks about "striking Jezebel's children dead," He's not threatening the false teacher's *biological* children. He's warning her *spiritual* children, those whom have aligned themselves with her teaching. As Greek scholar, Robert Mounce, says, "The children are those who have so unreservedly embraced the antinomian doctrines of their spiritual mother that they are best described as younger members of her family."[25] In other words, "Jezebel's *children*" are "Jezebel's *disciples*," those who have exchanged devotion to Jesus for the lie that we can follow Jesus *and* freely engage in sexual sin.

Jesus and Sexual Sin

It's important to understand that Jesus is not threatening those in the church who are stuck in sexual sin, but seeking to be free from that sin. He is confronting those who are promoting the lie that we can worship God AND engage in sexual sin, without needing to repent. Jesus is not *condemning* the *broken*; He's *confronting* the *brash*. He's warning those who have aligned themselves with Jezebel, who were saying: "I can worship God and express my sexuality however I want, whenever I want, with whomever I want."

That sounds strikingly similar to our culture's mantra on sexuality, doesn't it?

More concerning is how this is becoming the growing perspective of many in the Church – all in the name of *tolerance*. This is ironic, though, because the first thing Jesus calls out in the church at Thyatira are those who are *tolerating* Jezebel's false teaching about sex:

> "You tolerate that woman Jezebel, who calls herself a prophet. By her teaching she misleads my servants into sexual immorality…"
> ~ Revelation 2:20

Jesus does not tolerate those whose teaching leads others into sexual sin. He calls those teachers, "Jezebel." Not exactly a term of endearment. At the same time, there is no one more gracious with sexual sinners than Jesus. If you read through the Gospels, you cannot miss how compassionate Jesus is with those caught having sex outside of marriage.

Yes, Jesus spoke the truth of God's Word against sexual sin. But He was also gracious with those caught in sexual sin. Truth and Grace. Grace and Truth. Both. When the woman caught in adultery was brought before Jesus in John 8, He rescued her from execution, and then said two things to her: 1) I don't condemn you (Grace), and 2) Go and send no more (Truth).

That's who Jesus is. That's who we are to be, too: a people marked by truth *and* grace.

1) Proclaiming the **truth** about sexual sin – so that people understand their need to repent.
2) Cultivating environments of **grace** – so that people who repent are loved and accepted.

Tragically, many churches end up choosing truth OR grace.

Truth Churches

As followers of Jesus, we are to be bold in declaring that sex is a gift from God, designed for marriage between a man and woman, and that all other forms of sex outside that context is sin. Whether it's pre-marital, extra-marital, homosexual, polyamorous – we are to call it what God calls it: sin. Even if we get labeled haters and bigots, we are to hold fast to God's Word.

Proclaiming the truth of God's Word on this subject will cost us. There will be many outside the church (and a growing number inside the church) who will find this teaching backwards at best and hateful at worst. We need to be prepared for people to leave our churches. We need to be ready for societal backlash and lawsuits. Let's not get angry about it. And let's not get self-righteous about it. Let's just be ready for it. After all, Jesus said the world will hate us because of Him (Matthew 10:22). Let's not be shocked when His words are proven true.

Of course, if we're going to be people who love the truth, we can't just call out homosexual sex, or those particular sins for which we might not be tempted – so we can feel morally superior. We also need to call out and confess those places where *we've* missed the mark. Maybe I've never struggled with homosexuality, but can I say I've never looked at stuff I shouldn't have looked at? Can I say I've never stared too long at someone who wasn't my spouse? Can I say that my thought-life has been perfectly free of lust every moment of every day of my entire life? Jesus says if I've *ever* lusted, I am an adulterer (Matthew 5:28), which means I have no grounds to see myself as morally superior to anyone else. I, too, am a sexual sinner.

Holding to the truth of God's Word means getting real and going after *all* sin, starting with my own, which is why those in the church should be leading the way in confession and repentance. Unfortunately, in a lot of "truth churches" – when folks inside the church start getting honest about their sin (especially sexual sin), they're no longer welcome. Some "truth" churches are so proud of their reputation for not tolerating sin that they create an environment where no one gets honest about their sin (especially sexual sin) – because they're afraid if they come clean about it, they'll get kicked out. This fear is not without reason. It happens. I know a dating couple that was part of a "truth" church – until they confessed to having pre-marital sex. They were looking for help. But instead of being shown how to repent and take their sin to the cross, they were asked to leave the church. Of course, all that did was communicate to the rest of the church that they had better keep their sin hidden, unless they wanted to be kicked out, too.

It makes me want to puke when I hear those kinds of stories. I mean, what better place is there than the church to come clean with our brokenness, and ask for help? Didn't Jesus say that He came for the sick, not the healthy (Mark 2:17)? But this is what you find in churches that emphasize truth without grace: self-righteous judgmentalism.

Grace Churches

On the other hand, I know "grace" churches that pride themselves on being so tolerant – that in the name of grace – they refuse to call sin: sin. They don't want to make anyone feel bad or come across as judgmental. That's why a lot of churches don't even use words like *sin* or *repent* anymore.

I'm reminded of a church that hired a young woman to be their youth pastor, despite the fact that they knew she was living with her boyfriend, and had no intention of changing her lifestyle. I know this because my wife and I had a close relationship with this young woman after she came to faith in Christ. She was like a daughter to us. She was an incredibly bright and gifted young woman, with a desire to make a difference for Jesus in the world. There came a point, though, when she was unwilling to give up that which was competing with God for her heart. She didn't, at first, outright reject Jesus. She wanted Jesus *and*. So as the Scriptures charge me to do, I tried to correct her as clearly and gently as I knew how. But to no avail. She heard my heart, but it didn't change her mind.

The real issue for this young woman was not sex, but syncretism. She had made a deal with Jezebel: "that she could follow Jesus AND." She believed she could teach God's Word on Sunday AND do whatever she wanted the rest of the week. That's not even the most tragic part of the story, though. That came when I talked to the elders of the church where she was applying to be the youth pastor. I was one of her references, so they called me. As I shared my concerns about her lifestyle, though, they made it clear they didn't care what she did on her own time. They weren't prudish about sexual ethics. They just wanted to know about her gifts with students. What she did in her personal life was her business. They were a "grace" church. This is what you find in churches that emphasize grace without truth: syncretistic relativism.

JESUS' WORD TO THE CHURCH AT THYATIRA: REPENTANCE

The Son of God and Syncretistic Relativism

One of the reasons Jesus introduces Himself the way He does in this letter is to confront the spirit of syncretism that was there:

> "These are the words of the Son of God..."
> ~ Revelation 2:18

By introducing himself as *the* Son of God, Jesus is issuing a direct assault on moral relativism. If He is *the* Son of God, then it follows that *His* verdict about sin is not just one opinion among many. He is the One who defines what is right and wrong. This claim, though, flies in the face of our culture, where the idea of an objective standard of right and wrong is becoming increasingly unpopular. George Barna's research shows that, "72% of Americans between the ages of 18-25 believe there is no such thing as absolute truth." Even more concerning is that "this view appears to be shared by over half of those who claim to be born again Christians."[26]

No wonder it's so difficult to confront sin these days. Our culture (outside and inside the church) has embraced moral relativism. It's a religion. As Craig Keener says: "Much of our society has absolutized relativism (how is that for oxymoronic thinking?) as the only nonnegotiable truth, in essence arguing that *everyone is right unless one claims to be.*"[27]

This is what makes Jesus' claim at the outset of this letter so critical. If Jesus is *not* God, then we are free to ignore those parts of the Bible we don't like. But if Jesus *is* God, then no matter what society says is true (or what I feel is true), He is the One who defines what is true – including what is true in the sexual arena. Our response, as His followers, then, is to follow His lead – even if it means calling out and confessing that which our culture has endorsed as legitimate. Regardless of whether it's homosexuality, promiscuous heterosexuality, pornography, or any other sexual sin, we need to risk offending people by calling it what God calls it: sin. It may not feel very loving, but are we really loving our neighbors when we "reinterpret" God's Word to tickle their ears? No, we're hurting them, robbing them of the gift of repentance – by telling them that they don't need to.

True Love Means Telling People the Truth

That's the perspective of Rosaria Butterfield, a former tenured professor of English at Syracuse University. She was in a lesbian relationship, and deeply committed to the LGBT cause. Then, upon searching out the claims of Christianity, Rosaria came to believe Jesus is the Son of God. Immediately she realized the implications: she had to choose Jesus or her lifestyle. She knew it was either/or not both/and.

But that was 1999.

Today there are so-called Christian leaders promoting a version of Christianity where we can have Jesus AND express our sexual desires in whatever way *feels* right to us. This "progressive" sexual ethic masquerades as the more loving approach, but it's not, as Rosaria explains – in her open letter to a Christian leader, who declared that same sex marriage is acceptable before God:

> If this were 1999—the year that I was converted and walked away from the woman and lesbian community I loved—instead of 2016, [her] words about the holiness of LGBT relationships would have flooded into my world like a balm of Gilead. How amazing it would have been to have someone as radiant, knowledgeable, humble, kind, and funny as [her] saying out loud what my heart was shouting: *Yes, I can have Jesus and my girlfriend...* My emotional vertigo could find normal once again.
>
> Maybe I wouldn't need to lose everything to have Jesus. Maybe the gospel wouldn't ruin me while I waited, waited, waited for the Lord to build me

JESUS' WORD TO THE CHURCH AT THYATIRA: REPENTANCE

> back up after he convicted me of my sin, and I suffered the consequences. Maybe it would go differently for me than it did for Paul, Daniel, David, and Jeremiah. Maybe Jesus could save me without afflicting me. Maybe the Lord would give to me respectable crosses (Matthew 16:24). Manageable thorns (2 Corinthians 12:7).
>
> Today, I hear [her] words—words meant to encourage, not discourage, to build up, not tear down, to defend the marginalized, not broker unearned power—and a thin trickle of sweat creeps down my back. If I were still in the thick of the battle… [her] words would have put a millstone around my neck.[28]

Telling someone the truth is hard, but it's actually one of the most loving things we have to offer. Not telling someone the truth is like hanging a millstone around their neck.

Becoming a People of Truth and Grace

So how are we to respond to the moral relativism of our day without slipping into a self-righteous legalism? By pursuing truth *and* grace, not truth *or* grace. As Randy Alcorn writes:

> Truth without grace breeds a self-righteous legalism that poisons the church and pushes the world away from Christ. Grace without truth breeds moral indifference and keeps people from seeing their need for Christ. Attempts to 'soften' the gospel by minimizing *truth* keep people from Jesus. Attempts to 'toughen' the gospel by minimizing *grace* keep people from Jesus. It's not enough to offer grace *or* truth. We must offer both.[29]

Of course, transformation won't happen in our churches just because we subscribe to the *ideas* of truth and grace. Transformation happens in churches that are living out truth and grace in a way where others can *see* what it looks like in the messiness of real life. Churches that are experiencing Christ's transforming power are almost always marked by a few specific practices.

1) **Acknowledging our own sin and need for the Gospel**

Perhaps this one seems like a given, but it's not. Many churches give off an air that everyone in their religious club has their life all put together. This "spiritual arrival mentality" is one of the worst things that can happen to a church. How can people be set free from sin if there is the assumption that we're all okay? Newsflash: we're not all okay! Unfortunately, many churches are filled with people pretending to be more put together than they really are. As a result, very few of us are willing to risk getting honest about our sin. As Dietrich Bonhoeffer writes:

> The 'pious' fellowship permits no one to be a sinner. So everybody must conceal his sin. Many Christians are unthinkably horrified when a real sinner is suddenly discovered among the righteous. So we remain alone with our sin, living in lies and hypocrisy. But the fact is we are sinners… It is the grace of the Gospel, which is so hard for the pious to understand, that confronts us with the truth and says: 'You are a sinner, a great, desperate sinner; now come, as the sinner that you are, to God who loves you.'[30]

It's only when we're willing to get honest about the truth of our own sin and personal need for God's grace that we can be transformed by the gospel.

JESUS' WORD TO THE CHURCH AT THYATIRA: REPENTANCE

2) **Modeling transparency and confession**

Someone has to go first. It's not easy to get honest about our sin and shortcomings, but when we do so, it inspires transparency and confession in others. It's contagious. I've watched this happen among students. I've witnessed it in adult small groups. I've even experienced it in corporate worship services following the preaching of God's Word. When I risk lacing my sermons with personal confession, modeling what it looks like for me to repent of *my sins* – it's far more effective in inspiring repentance than when I simply tell people to repent of *their sins*.

3) **Regularly hearing testimonies of transformation**

Few things inspire confession and repentance like a testimony from someone who used to be bound by some sin, who has found forgiveness and freedom in Christ. One of the highlights for me as a pastor is the transformation stories I've heard in corporate worship services:

- Jesus delivering people from the snare of pornography and other sexual sins
- Jesus setting people free from alcoholism and drug addictions
- Jesus empowering people to forgive those who hurt them
- Jesus giving courage to people to start sharing their faith
- Jesus inspiring people to step out of their comfort zone to serve
- Jesus helping people to trust Him with their money
- Jesus healing people of guilt and shame who have had abortions

Testimonies inspire people to turn to Jesus and trust Him with their sin and shame. It's one thing for a pastor to preach about how Jesus *can* forgive and transform. It's another thing to hear stories of it happening in the lives of real people. For example,

I'm reminded of the great work God did in many hearts on the Sunday morning Irene shared this testimony:

> *I will never forget the day the Lord set me free from sexual sin and the shame of my past. The message that Sunday was about Jesus calming the storm when His disciples were afraid. A revelation came to me that day. I realized Jesus has authority over everything. Everything! I saw that there is nothing Jesus cannot conquer. I realized that day that as long as I was holding onto Jesus' hand, nothing could make me fall back into the sexual sin I had fallen into so many times in the past. Up until that day, the enemy had me paralyzed with fear, telling me there were certain things I could never be free from. And I believed him. But that Sunday, I knew it was a lie, because Jesus has authority over everything. I could be free.*
>
> *I knew I could not get there on my own, though. I knew I had to confess my past and my fear of falling back into sexual sin, so I shared it with a prayer counselor and one of our pastors. I've since learned that once we share our sin or our weakness with someone, it is no longer a secret that the enemy can hold over us. Satan's power is lessened when we bring our sin out of the darkness and into the light.*
>
> *For two years now I have been free of all areas of sexual sin. I'm learning that Jesus wants me to be a walking testimony of His greatness. It's not about religion. It's not about going to church and putting on a front and acting as if everything is okay. It's all about a relationship with Jesus. The more I spend time with Him, the more I begin to look like Him. The more I get to know His heart, the more I want to get rid of the sin in my life.*

> *I used to be embarrassed to talk about my past bondage to sexual sin. But now I'm not. Jesus has set me free, free of my sexual sin and free of condemnation. The enemy wanted me to be ashamed so I would not share about my deliverance, but now I understand that through my testimony, many will find freedom in Jesus. I refuse to stand by and allow the enemy to continue to keep my brothers and sisters captive. May the Lord use me however He wants. I belong to Him and only Him!*

The Lord worked powerfully through Irene's testimony. At the close of both services – the front of the worship center was filled with people, repenting of their sins (of all kinds), sharing their burdens with prayer counselors, and turning to Jesus for forgiveness and freedom.

Repentance: The New Norm

One of my hopes for the American church is that repentance wouldn't be this awkward thing we avoid because we're concerned what people will think about us. How beautiful would it be if repentance and bringing our sin to the cross was a regular feature of our church life? That's what Jesus was reaching for in Thyatira. It's what He's still reaching for today.

That young woman, who was like a daughter to us, eventually stopped following Jesus altogether. She married an atheist, got her PhD, and landed a great job. For the next several years, she thought she had life by the tail; that she had evolved beyond all of that simplistic, primitive religion warning against things like sin. And then her life came crashing down like a house of cards when her husband left her. God used that pain, though, to bring her back to Himself. This past New Year's Day, she came to visit – to tell us, in person, the story of how God had used that pain to humble her, convict her of her sin, and bring her back to Christ. Amanda and I were in tears as we listened to her testimony of God's grace. Her story was marked by a lot of hardship and heartache, but her demeanor was marked by peace and joy as she talked about how God graciously used that pain to draw her heart back to Himself.

That's the heart behind Jesus calling the church at Thyatira to "repent" three times in this letter (Rev 2:21-22). It's because He wants His people to experience this kind of transforming grace. And the only way to access this transforming grace is through the doorway of repentance.

So why is this kind of repentance so rare in most churches?

Pastoral Confession

It might sound crazy to some, but I believe we pastors are the ones most responsible for a lack of repentance. Too often, out of concern for being seeker-sensitive, we're not clear that becoming a Christian is about more than just getting our sins forgiven so we can go to Heaven when we die. It's also about entrusting the leadership of our life to Jesus, and submitting ourselves to whatever His Word says – even the unpopular, counter-cultural parts of His Word, like the letter to the church at Thyatira.

Sometimes I think we're so concerned to make Jesus look appealing to our culture – that we cheapen the gospel – saying that all He wants is to be a *part* of your life. Whatever happened to: "For those of you who want to become a Christian, here's the invitation: 'Take up your cross, die to yourself, and give your life to Christ'" (Mark 8:34-35). That's the invitation Jesus gave.

Sometimes pastors shy away from issuing that invitation because we don't want to scare people away with a message that sounds too hard or harsh. I get it. We have new people coming to our church every week. I don't want to offend them right out of the gate. I want to do that later.

I'm kidding.

It's never my goal to offend. But if I'm going to be true to preaching all of God's Word – there will be times when I offend people. To put a sharper point on it, there will be times when

JESUS' WORD TO THE CHURCH AT THYATIRA: REPENTANCE

God's Word offends people, because God's Word is an equal opportunity offender. There's something in there that will offend everyone at some point. But it's my job to lay it out there anyway – even in a culture that is hyper-sensitive to offense. Otherwise, by neglecting the parts of the Bible that might potentially make people mad – I'm acting as if I know better than God does what people need to hear. Talk about arrogant. Sadly, I've been guilty of it, treating Jesus like He's some religious product that needs my slick salesmanship if anyone is going to want to follow Him. Instead, what I should be doing is proclaiming the greatness of our crucified and resurrected Lord, declaring that His sacrifice is so amazing and His coming Kingdom so glorious – that we would be fools to not repent and submit ourselves completely to Him and His Word!

That's our message – at least it should be.

Kyle Idleman has an analogy for pastors who emphasize the benefits of Christianity, but neglect the call to take up our cross and follow Jesus. He says it's like a dad who advertises incentives to anyone out there interested in marrying his daughter:

> Imagine that my daughter isn't married but she really wants to be. I decide I'm going to help make that happen. So, I take out an ad in the newspaper, put up a billboard sign, and make T-shirts *begging* someone to *choose* her. I even offer some attractive gifts as incentives. Doesn't that cheapen who my daughter is? Wouldn't that make it seem that whoever came to her would be doing her a favor? I would never do that to my daughter. I would set the standard high. I would do background checks and lie detector tests. There would be lengthy applications that must be filled out in triplicate. References would be checked and hidden cameras installed. If you want to have a relationship with my daughter, you better be prepared to give her the best of everything you have. I don't want

to just hear you say that you love her; I want to know that you are COMMITTED to her. I want to know that you would give your LIFE for her.31

I have a picture of my three daughters on the front screen of my phone. I'm looking at it right now, trying to imagine offering free t-shirts and other incentives to anyone "willing" to marry one of my precious little girls. Are you kidding me? The analogy breaks down, but sometimes we pastors – in our sincere desire to make Christianity look more appealing to our culture – communicate the gospel in a way that makes it sound like we're doing God a favor by becoming a follower of His Son. We end up sending the message that Jesus is so hard up for followers that we have to emphasize the benefits of Christianity and downplay the costs. The message then becomes that you can receive God's forgiveness without Jesus interfering with your life. In other words, you can worship God *and* still do whatever you want. That's the spirit of Jezebel.

That's the spirit that infiltrated the church at Thyatira. And that's the spirit that's infiltrated many churches in America. And it's largely because pastors, who are unwilling to call people to repent, are sending a message that we can have a relationship with Jesus *and* still "see other people."

But Jesus won't have it.

Jesus is a Jealous Lover

When Amanda walks into my office, she sees her picture on my desk. It's a symbol of my love for her. It's a sign of my exclusive commitment to her. But what if, as she looked around my office, she spotted pictures of other women, too? I can tell you, in no uncertain terms, that it would not matter if I said, "But Sweetheart, I love you the *most*. You're *first* in my life. You're my *favorite*. Those other women I *like*, but you I *love*." That answer would not cut it. Why? Because Amanda is not interested in being the "first among many." She wants, and deserves, to be the "one and only."32

In an even more intensely exclusive way, Jesus, who introduces himself in this letter as *"the* Son of God" (2:18), refuses to share us with other lovers. Not because He's narcissistic or insecure, but because He's appropriately jealous, the way Amanda would be appropriately jealous – if she saw my heart wandering toward some other woman.

That's why Jesus goes after Jezebel and this false teaching so zealously. He's doing so because He loves us. He's doing so because He's protecting our relationship. He knows what will happen if He just stands by passively and does nothing, while we dupe ourselves into believing Jezebel's lie that we can have our cherished sin, and still have a relationship with Him.

Jesus will not tolerate that lie.

I'm not saying Jesus expects us to never sin once we become His follower. I would be dead meat if that were the case, and so would you. But Jesus does call us to confess and repent of our sin when we blow it. He calls us to turn back to Him when we fall short, so that we don't fall prey to making agreements with Jezebel, believing that it's not that big a deal if we worship God *and*. Jesus is not interested in sharing you with other lovers. He's not content to *date* you, while you "see other people." It's marriage or nothing with Jesus. And anyone who's been led to believe Jesus is okay with any other arrangement has been duped by the spirit of Jezebel.

That's why I twinge when I hear pastors give invitations that make it sound like Jesus is pleading with you to let Him be *part* of your life, as if His endgame is to have access to a little corner of *your* existence so He can help *you* with *your* agenda. Sometimes pastors make it sound like Jesus wants to be your butler or personal assistant, someone committed to helping you with whatever you need – whether that's making more money, finding a husband, experiencing less emotional anxiety, or getting you whatever it is that you want out of life. But Jesus is not looking to be *part* of your life. You can't find a single verse in the Bible where Jesus asks someone to let Him be a *part* of their lives. Jesus wants to be in *charge* of your life. But that message flies in the face of a culture where people want to call themselves Christians *and* still do whatever they want.

Flexitarian Spirituality

This reminds me of people who like to call themselves vegetarians, but who still want to eat meat. J.M. Hirsch of the Associated Press wrote an article about this group of people several years ago. Here's an excerpt of it:

> After five years, Christy Pugh has no trouble sticking to her vegetarian regimen. "The secret to her success?" Hirsch asks. "Eating meat."
>
> "Sometimes I feel like I'm a bad vegetarian, like I'm not strict enough or good enough," Pugh said. "I really like vegetarian food; I'm just not 100% committed."
>
> Pugh is part of a growing group of people who eat vegetarian, but make exceptions from time to time. In other words, they don't eat meat, unless they really like it. "I usually eat vegetarian," Pugh says, "but I really like sausage." 33

What's fascinating about this story is what came next: the real vegetarians got angry about this new group of meat-eating vegetarians – for calling themselves vegetarians! So they put pressure on these pseudo-vegetarians to change their name. And they did. The name they came up with for themselves? "Flexitarians." It's a word that gives options. It means Christy can be a vegetarian *and* still eat sausage. Flexitarianism is now a multi-million dollar business, catering to those who want to be vegetarian *and* still eat meat.

Incidentally, this word, "flexitarian," was recently voted most useful word of the year by the American Dialect Society. That is quite the commentary on our culture. We are a flexitarian culture. We love to keep our options open. Flexitarian is also an apt word for much of the American church, which is a billion dollar business, with many of its leaders catering to those who want to follow Jesus *and* still do whatever they want.

What Are You Holding Out of the Water?

Perhaps the best illustration of this syncretistic, Jezebel-spirit is found at the end of Kyle Idleman's book, *Not A Fan*. It's a story about a strange baptism practice that the church allowed, centuries ago, when knights wanted to be baptized:

> When the church would baptize one of the knights, they would be baptized with their sword, *but they wouldn't take their swords under the water with them.* Instead they would hold their swords up out of the water while the rest of them would be immersed. It was the knights' way of saying, "Jesus, you can have control of all of me, except this. I'm all yours, Jesus, except for what I do on the battlefield. How I use this sword, that's not part of the deal. I'm all yours, Jesus, except for this."[34]

That pretty well describes the believers at Thyatira. They were *mostly* following Jesus. I mean, Jesus had plenty for which to commend them:

> "I know your deeds, your love and faith, your service and perseverance, and that you are now doing more than you did at first."
> ~ Revelation 2:19

It's not like the church at Thyatira was filled with a bunch of Satan-worshippers, who wanted nothing to do with Jesus. They were Christians. They even received commendation from Jesus for how they were growing in love, faith, perseverance, and good works. They were mostly "in" with Jesus. But Jesus didn't want "mostly in." He wanted "all in." And they weren't all in. They had a blind spot when it came to sexual sin. They wanted to be baptized into Jesus, as long as they could hold that one area of their lives out of the water.

A lot of us approach our relationship with God like that. We want Jesus to be a *part* of our lives, but we don't want Him to take *over* our lives. We want Jesus *in* our lives, but we don't want Him *interfering* with our lives. We want Him to *bless* our lives, but we don't want Him to *mess* with our lives.

Jesus won't have us that way, though. Just like He wanted all of the church at Thyatira, He wants all of us, too. He refuses to share us, His Bride, with any other lovers.

Jesus' Promise to the Church at Thyatira

It's interesting what Jesus promises the church at Thyatira, if they will turn back to Him, break off agreements they've made with Jezebel, and serve Him alone:

> "To the one who overcomes, I will give the Morning Star."
> ~ Revelation 2:28

What does it mean that Jesus will give us the Morning Star? Revelation is a tricky book to interpret, but in many cases, the book actually interprets itself. The final chapter of Revelation explains this seemingly obscure promise:

> "I, Jesus, have sent my angel to give you this testimony for the churches. I am the Root and Offspring of David, and the bright Morning Star."
> ~ Revelation 22:16

JESUS' WORD TO THE CHURCH AT THYATIRA: REPENTANCE

Jesus is the Morning Star.

In other words, Jesus promises Himself. Jesus promises that — despite the times we've spurned Him, chasing after other lovers — if we'll confess our sin, repent, and *turn* back to Him, He will give us Himself. Like the husband who has betrayed his wife, he knows the difference between being *forgiven* by his wife (which is wonderful), and his wife giving *herself* to him again. It's the difference between forgiveness, which is good, and restored relationship, which is even better.

And that's what Jesus is offering. That's how much He loves His Bride, us, His church. No matter what we've done, or how dark or deep our betrayal — Jesus' shed blood on the cross was (and is) sufficient to both forgive us, and restore us back to Himself.

But He wants all of us.

Not all of us, except our sword — *all* of us
Not all of us, except our checkbook — *all* of us
Not all of us, except what we look at on our computer — *all* of us
Not all of us, except that one relationship — *all* of us
Not all of us, except our entertainment world — *all* of us
Not all of us, except our social media — *all* of us
Not all of us, except that secret sin — *all* of us
Not all of us, except that thing I've rationalized — *all* of us

Jesus is a Jealous Lover. He will not share us with other lovers. At the same time, there's never been a more forgiving Lover than Jesus. Even after we've messed up and messed around, Jesus says: "If you'll repent and turn back to Me, I'll not only forgive you. I'll give you Myself."

Responding to Jesus' Letter

1) Confess any agreements you've made with Jezebel, naming that thing you've been "holding up out of the water": _____, and then surrendering it to Jesus.

2) Rejoice that as you turn from this idol and turn to Jesus, He not only forgives you, He frees you from its power, and promises you more of Himself.

3) Share your testimony of taking this step. It doesn't mean you'll be perfect from now on, but verbalizing your repentance diminishes Jezebel's power in your life, and points others to the transforming grace of Jesus.

JESUS' WORD TO THE CHURCH AT THYATIRA: REPENTANCE

Digging Deeper

1) Read *Not a Fan* (by Kyle Idleman) – a book that describes the lack of commitment to Jesus in the American Church, and then outlines what it looks like to be devoted to Him.

2) Read *The Secret Thoughts of an Unlikely Convert: An English Professor's Journey into Christian Faith* (by Rosaria Butterfield) – a powerful book that details Rosaria's conversion to Christ.

3) Read *Is God Anti-Gay* (by Sam Allberry) – a short, powerful book, written by a pastor who is same-sex attracted, and committed to what God's Word says regarding sex being reserved for a man and woman in the context of marriage.

6

JESUS' WORD TO THE CHURCH AT SARDIS: REMEMBER

THE HUMAN BRAIN HAS THE CAPACITY TO store vast amounts of information. If it were possible to make a copy of everything that was in an average adult's brain, it would take approximately 3.2 million DVDs to hold it all. And yet I can't remember the sermon from last Sunday – and I preached it. Our memory problem is not a matter of storage. It's a matter of recall. We can only recall about 2-3% of what's located on our brain's memory hard drive. That's why we get frustrated when we forget things we know are stored in there, like the names of people, birthdates and anniversaries, or where we put our car keys or phone!

We're like the elderly couple that started forgetting things. They were so concerned that they went to see their doctor. But after running a series of tests, the doctor told them they were fine; they were just experiencing "senior moments." He did give them some advice about their memory lapses: he encouraged them to start writing things down.

Later that night, after watching television, the husband got up from his chair. His wife asked, "Where are you going?"

"To the kitchen," he replied.

"While you're there, would you get me a bowl of ice cream?" she asked.

"Sure."

"Well, don't you think you should write it down so you remember it?"

"No, I can remember it," he assured her. "You want a bowl of ice cream."

"Well, I would also like some strawberries on top. You had better write that down because I know you'll forget it," she said.

"I can remember that. You want a bowl of ice cream with strawberries."

"I'd also like whip cream on top. You'll forget that. You had better write it down."

With irritation in his voice, he said, "I don't need to write that down. I can remember it. You want ice cream with strawberries and whip cream on top."

Twenty minutes later, he returned from the kitchen, and handed his wife a plate of bacon and eggs. She stared at the plate. Exasperated, she finally broke her silence: "See, I knew you wouldn't remember… Where's my toast?"

Memory lapses, when they're about ice cream or toast, are humorous. But there are other times when forgetting is not funny at all. Diseases like Alzheimer's and Dementia are tragic because losing our memories is a form of losing our lives.

We don't want to forget.

God doesn't want us to forget, either. Maybe that's why the word, "remember," is mentioned 168 times in the Bible. God doesn't want us to forget what He's done for us, what He's taught us, or what He's called us to. But we are prone to forget, aren't we?

Haven't you had experiences where God showed you something, taught you something, or came through for you in some powerful way, and you said to yourself, *I will never let the memory of this lesson or experience fade* – but over time, it did?

I have. I'm not the only one. As John Eldredge writes:

> Virtually every person I've ever counseled follows a similar pattern. Over the course of our time together, some wonderful things begin to happen. Not necessarily at first, and never on command, but God shows up. The lights turn on for these people; their heart is lifted; grateful tears flow. Suddenly, faith, hope, and love seem the only way to live. And I nearly dread the next session. When they return the following week, it is as though it never happened. That marvelous day is a distant memory…All is forgotten…I want to grab them and shake them into sense, shouting, 'Don't you remember? Why did you let it slip away?'[35]

God has been teaching Amanda and me a lot about the importance of remembering. The more we reflect on what He's done for us, the more inspired we are to follow Him. This lesson has been so significant that if Amanda wasn't afraid of needles, she'd get a tattoo that says, *Remember*, as a visual reminder of all God has done for her.

I think that's the one-word tattoo Jesus would have inked onto the church at Sardis, too.

The believers there had forgotten what Jesus had done for them and what He had called them to. Despite a rich history and legacy as a church, they had fallen asleep spiritually. And the way Jesus woke them up was not by telling them any new information, but by jogging their memory. As C.S. Lewis said, "Sometimes Christians need more to be reminded than instructed."[36]

That's exactly what the church at Sardis needed: to be reminded of what Jesus had done for them, to be reminded of all that Jesus had taught them, and to be reminded of all that Jesus had called them to. Of course, the believers in Sardis aren't the only ones who need their memories jogged. Being reminded of what Jesus has said or done for us is often the very thing that will wake us up from a spiritual slumber. For those of us who have a tendency toward spiritual amnesia, Jesus' word, REMEMBER, is His word for us, too.

"To the angel of the church in Sardis write: These are the words of him who holds the seven spirits of God and the seven stars. I know your deeds; you have a reputation of being alive, but you are dead. Wake up! Strengthen what remains and is about to die, for I have found your deeds unfinished in the sight of my God. Remember, therefore, what you have received and heard; hold it fast, and repent. But if you do not wake up, I will come like a thief, and you will not know at what time I will come to you.

Yet you have a few people in Sardis who have not soiled their clothes. They will walk with me, dressed in white, for they are worthy. The one who is victorious will, like them, be dressed in white. I will never blot out the name of that person from the book of life, but will acknowledge that name before my Father and his angels. Whoever has ears, let them hear what the Spirit says to the churches."

~ Revelation 3:1-6

Historical Context: Spiritual Atrophy

Whereas most churches in the first century faced opposition from the society around them, the church at Sardis didn't. Whereas many churches had to deal with false teachers infiltrating their ranks and promoting heresy and immorality, the church at Sardis didn't. Darrell Johnson writes: "Unlike the other churches of the Roman province of Asia, the church at Sardis was not under pressure. They were not having to face persecution."[37]

According to scholars, it didn't cost much to be a follower of Jesus in Sardis. The city leaders were very accommodating of Christianity.

JESUS' WORD TO THE CHURCH AT SARDIS: REMEMBER

That sounds like a good thing. And in some ways it was a blessing. But it also created a problem for the church: *spiritual atrophy.*

In the physical realm, we know we need resistance to maintain muscle. Otherwise atrophy sets in, like what happens to astronauts in space without the resistance of gravity. Studies have shown that astronauts can lose up to twenty percent of their muscle mass on a single week-long spaceflight. That can be a real danger if an astronaut has to perform a strenuous emergency procedure upon re-entering the Earth's gravitational field. The only way to minimize muscle atrophy in space is through intensive exercise. This is why astronauts on the International Space Station typically spend over two hours a day exercising. If astronauts aren't intentional about working their muscles in space, it can cost them their lives.[38]

This principle is true in the spiritual realm, too. If we're not facing adversity, if there's no tension, if life is always smooth sailing, we'll lose our spiritual muscles. We'll get soft and sleepy. That's what happened to the church at Sardis. They looked like a strong church. They had a good "reputation" (v1). But they had become so comfortable in their accommodating culture, they fell asleep, which is why Jesus begins his letter to them with those alarm clock words: "Wake up!" (v2).

Comfort can be a gift. But too much comfort can be a death sentence. This is not only true in space, and in the spiritual arena, but at the biological level, too. John Ortberg describes an experiment that was done at the University of California at Berkeley, which involved putting an amoeba into an absolutely stress-free environment.

> The temperature was perfect; there was just the precise concentration of moisture; food was constantly supplied; the amoeba's surroundings were such that it had to make no adjustments at all to survive. Whatever it is that might give a little amoeba high blood pressure or ulcers was removed. Everything a little amoeba could ever want was at its beck and call. Do you know what happened to that little amoeba? It died. [39]

That's what happened to the church at Sardis: too much comfort. And it killed them. The church looked alive. They had a great reputation. But Jesus said, "You're dead" (v1).

The Prosperity Test

It's interesting that the only two churches that failed to receive words of commendation are the two that didn't face persecution: Sardis and Laodicea. This is not to say Jesus loves persecuted Christians more than He loves those who are not being persecuted. It wasn't their fault they weren't experiencing adversity. Neither was it their fault that they were living in what one commentator called a "fabulously wealthy" city.40 Jesus doesn't rebuke them for their comfort or money. He rebukes them for allowing their comfortable lifestyle to lead them to fall asleep spiritually, to where they became a social club, merely going through the motions of church.

Comfort, safety and prosperity can be blessings. But they can also be tests. Sometimes the test of *prosperity* is more difficult to pass than the test of *persecution*. As one Romanian church leader said, "In my experience, 95% of believers, who face the test of persecution, pass it; 95% of believers who face the test of prosperity, fail it." The church at Sardis was failing the prosperity test. Their wealth wasn't inspiring greater faith or more diligent service. It wasn't motivating them to take risks for the Kingdom. It was leading them to apathy. It's why Jesus called their deeds, "incomplete", or as some translations say, "unfinished" (v2).

This is where there's a haunting parallel between the church at Sardis and the church in America. We, too, find ourselves in a culture marked by incredible wealth and comfort. It shouldn't be a surprise, then, that spiritual apathy tends to characterize many of us and our churches, too.

But this doesn't mean it's our fate to become spiritually dead. Like astronauts who have learned to exercise in a context without gravity, there are things we can do to exercise our spiritual muscles in a context of prosperity. We may not be facing overt persecution or extreme poverty, but that doesn't mean we can't find ways

JESUS' WORD TO THE CHURCH AT SARDIS: REMEMBER

to identify with those who are. And in my experience, the more intentional I am about identifying with those who are enduring persecution or poverty – the more God wakes me up.

That's one of the reasons I'm so thankful to be part of a ministry serving widows and orphans in Burundi. Not just for what I can do to help *them*, but for what the Lord does in *me* as I identify with their adversity – even in small ways. For example, a few years ago, our family did a simplicity-fast. It consisted of eating the same simple foods every day, as a way of identifying with the Burundian widows, who eat the same thing (and very little) every day. Eating that way for one month allowed us to save enough to support another Burundian widow in her journey toward spiritual healing and financial self-sufficiency.[41]

To be honest, I didn't love the fast. After weeks of eating split pea soup every day, I was ready for a cheeseburger (or two). But it was a powerful experience for our entire family. Jesus did something in *us* as we identified with *others*. Two weeks into the fast, we gathered as a family to share with each other what Jesus was teaching us. Karis, my (then) twelve year old, shared about sitting down in the school cafeteria, and seeing her friends with fun foods in their lunches. At first, she said it made her think about what she didn't have. But then she decided to use that desire for comfort food as a trigger to pray for the widows in Burundi. Every time she found herself craving a food that one of her peers was enjoying, she took a moment to silently pray for the widows. As I listened to my daughter share what Jesus was teaching her through this fast, I thought to myself, *Wow, this is what Jesus does in us when we identify with those who are truly experiencing adversity.*

Ask Jesus if He has some way for you to identify with those who are experiencing adversity – not only for the *good* that could result for them, but for the *growth* that could result for you.

- Maybe by praying for those in need
- Maybe by fasting and giving the money you save to a ministry serving the poor
- Maybe by serving with a group ministering to the disabled

- Maybe by hosting the homeless or marginalized in your home for a meal
- Maybe by going to those in need – either locally or on the other side of the world

Not just for the good we can do for *them*, but for what God will do in *us*.

This is the kind of intentionality we need to have when facing the prosperity test – so that we don't end up like the church at Sardis, falling asleep because we're too comfortable.

The Freedom Test

The church in Sardis also enjoyed the freedom of religion. Unlike the believers in Smyrna, who were kicked out of the synagogue, the Christians in Sardis were accepted by the Jews. This is significant, because it meant they got in on the Jewish exemption clause of not having to worship the emperor. Jews and Christians weren't just *tolerated* in Sardis; they were *celebrated*. They had the same rights and privileges as all of the other religious and civic groups of the city. They were even allowed to build a huge synagogue right next to the city gymnasium, the epicenter of Roman society. It stood as a testimony to the status of the Judeo-Christian community in Sardis. The believers enjoyed something like our first amendment right to worship freely. This sounds like a blessing (and it was), but it also led to a problem: *pride,* a patriotic pride where they saw themselves first as citizens of the great city of Sardis, and only second as citizens of God's Kingdom.

I can understand that kind of patriotic pride. If I had been a Christian in the first century, I would have wanted to live in Sardis. Who wouldn't want that kind of freedom? I've been to places in the world where communist regimes ruled or where dictators were in charge. I've seen what living in those countries can mean for Christians. I'm thankful for the freedoms I enjoy as a citizen of the United States. But the temptation is to slip into entitlement regarding this religious freedom, instead of seeing it as a window of opportunity God is giving me to share Christ without fear of persecution – knowing that this may not be the case forever.

Religious freedom is a gift, but not for us. It's a gift for those who still need Jesus.

What's ironic (and tragic) is that we who enjoy this religious freedom, are often less inclined to share the gospel than those who are persecuted for doing so. Sometimes we, myself included, take for granted that we can share Jesus whenever we want to, and so we wait for the "perfect" time to do so. But rarely does the "perfect" time present itself. Thus, we keep waiting.

Perhaps we would do well to take a page out of the playbook of the persecuted church in Southeast Asia, from believers who do not enjoy the same religious freedom we do. On the first day they come to faith in Christ, they're told to do three things:

1) Make a list of every unbeliever they know
2) Circle the names of the ten people on that list who are least likely to kill them if they speak to them about Christ
3) Go share Christ with those ten people as soon as possible [42]

That's their church growth strategy. So let me ask: Do you have ten people in your life, who don't yet follow Jesus, who won't kill you if you share your faith with them?

I'm convicted by that question. I mean, how much more should we be sharing Christ – given the freedom we have (for now) to do so? If we want to pass the freedom test, we need to view the freedom we have, not as a gift for us, but as a gift for those who still need Jesus.

The Security Test

Perhaps the greatest point of pride for Sardis was their military might. Their city's defense seemed impenetrable. Scholar, Gottfried Osei, paints the picture: "Sardis was built on a rocky promontory with sheer sides all round, except for a narrow strip of land linking it to the rest of the countryside which was easily guarded."43

It seemed impossible for an enemy to invade their city.

And yet, as much as the people of Sardis saw themselves as invincible, twice in their own history (once in 549 BC and again in 218 BC) their enemies were able to defeat them by covert attacks at night, while those who were supposed to keep watch, fell asleep. Osei writes, "Under the cover of darkness they penetrated the defenses, and twice by this method Sardis was conquered and taken by enemies."44

As much as the people of Sardis prided themselves on being invincible, they weren't.

Here's why this history lesson is significant. It seems this false sense of security had crept into the *church* at Sardis, which is why Jesus uses 'thief in the night' imagery to try to wake His people up from their complacency:

> "If you do not wake up, I will come like a thief, and you will not know at what time I will come to you."
> ~ Revelation 3:3

Jesus knew Sardis' history, so He spoke to them with a painful metaphor He knew they'd understand. Not to motivate them to shore up their military position, but to shore up their spiritual position. He wanted them to wake up and stay on guard against the temptations of comfort, wealth, and apathy that were sneaking in and destroying their faith.

Jesus is not promoting a works-righteousness, where we have to "do more" to earn our spiritual security. He is confronting an apathy that can result from a misunderstanding about spiritual security. So many Christians have this misguided notion of eternal security, that once we've prayed a prayer or gotten baptized, or become a church member, we're now eternally "secure" – and therefore can now go on our merry way, living life however we want to. But that's a miscarriage of the idea of eternal security.

Let me be clear: when we believe the gospel and put our trust in Christ, we can rest assured that our sins are forgiven and we are right with God. But the gift of assurance was never intended to be an excuse for spiritual apathy. The faith that saves is the faith that perseveres, which is why Jesus says it's those who are victorious whose "names will never be blotted out of the Book of Life" (Rev 3:5).

The faith that saves is the faith that perseveres. That's what we need to remember if we're going to pass the security test, and not be taken out by spiritual complacency.

The Reputation Test

One of the temptations for many second generation churches is that it lives off the reputation of a previous generation that was sold out for Jesus. That's what was happening in Sardis. It's why Jesus says to them, "you have a *reputation* of being alive" (Rev 3:1). As Osei-Mensah writes:

> At one time in its history, the church in Sardis had real saints who stood firm for the Lord Jesus Christ, and whose shining testimony became known in the locality… But alas, that generation had gone on to their reward, and a different generation had arisen in the church which still bore the name and cashed in on the reputation and fame of the former generation. But they did not show the same faith and faithfulness toward the Lord.[45]

The church at Sardis still *looked* impressive. They met in one of the biggest buildings in the city. Financially, they were strong. Socially, they had status. But spiritually, Jesus says: *You're dead. You look alive, but you're just living off the reputation of a previous generation.*

I don't want to paint with too broad a brush stroke, but there are parallels between the church at Sardis and some churches (and denominations) in America, which are living off the reputation of a previous generation. Don't get me wrong: the church in America is still making a huge Kingdom-difference around the world. But today there are actually missionaries being sent to *us* from other nations. After decades of relative prosperity, comfort and safety, many of our church's spiritual muscles have atrophied. We've grown complacent about our calling, leaving "unfinished" (Rev 3:2) the Great Commission that Christ has called us to.

There's nothing inherently wrong with enjoying prosperity or religious freedom. These can be incredible blessings. But if we're not careful, they can also become distractions that keep us from following Jesus with the kind of holy abandon that marked earlier generations. Erwin McManus, in *Chasing Daylight*, explains how this can happen:

> The more God blesses your life, the more you have to lose. The more you have to lose, the more you have to risk. The more you have to risk, the higher the price of following God. In some twisted way, God's blessings to us can become our greatest hindrances…When my wife and I were in our twenties, had no kids, no house, nothing to tie us down it was easy to respond to even the slightest prompting of God's Spirit inviting us to a new challenge. After all, we were not much more than educated nomads. Everything we treasured was essentially contained in our relationship. There was really very little else to consider. But then God *blessed* me with a job, and then He *blessed* us with [kids]. Then He *blessed* us with a new house. Did I mention the new car and all the great furniture? After ten years of sacrificial ministry, it seemed as if the floodgates of heaven had been opened to us in terms of earthly possessions. Then God's voice came again, inviting us to a new journey, calling us to a new adventure. It sounded wonderful, but there were a few minor glitches to

> the invitation. The job would have to go, the house would have to go, the retirement would have to go, our savings would have to go, and most of the really cool stuff would have to go. We were allowed to keep the kids... It is not an understatement to say that God's blessings were like an anchor around our ankles. We had received them as we walked with God, yet now they had the potential of paralyzing us and robbing us of the divine moments before us.46

The church at Sardis was blessed, but those blessings had become like anchors around their ankles, keeping them from following Jesus with the same holy abandon that marked an earlier generation. And it only takes one generation for a vital church to die. As Osei-Mensah writes: "Spiritual deadness is the particular peril of the second and third generation church."47

That's one of the reasons this letter is so important for us today. It's especially applicable for those of us who have grown up in the church, and for those of us who have kids or grandkids. If we don't intentionally pass down to the next generation a passionate devotion to Jesus and a deep commitment to His Kingdom, they'll become like the church at Sardis, having a reputation of being alive, but being spiritually dead. Lord Jesus, help us.

The Key: Remember!

Jesus' letter is a hard word to hear. Nobody wants to be told they're spiritually dead. That feels so final and hopeless. But let's not forget that Jesus is in the resurrection business. Jesus can resurrect spiritually dead churches, spiritually dead families, and spiritually dead individuals. The key to spiritual resurrection is His word to the church at Sardis: remember.

> "Remember, therefore, what you have received and heard..."
> ~ Revelation 3:3

God isn't always looking to give us *new* information or *new* instructions. Sometimes He simply calls us to *remember* what we've already received and heard. This is a pattern in the Old Testament, too. After God rescued His people out of slavery to Egypt, His primary message to them was to *remember* what He had done for them:

- "Watch yourselves closely so that you do not forget the things your eyes have seen or let them slip from your heart as long as you live. Teach them to your children and to their children after them. Remember…" (Dt 4:9-10)
- "Do not be afraid… remember well what the Lord your God did to Pharaoh and to all Egypt…" (Dt 7:18)
- "When you have eaten and are satisfied, praise the Lord your God for the good land He has given you. Be careful that you do not forget the Lord… Otherwise, when you eat and are satisfied, when you build fine houses and settle down… your heart will become proud and you will forget the Lord your God, who brought you out of Egypt… Remember the Lord…" (Dt 8:10-14, 18)

God could not have been clearer with His people about the importance of remembering what He had done for them. Still, once the memory of His rescue began to fade into the background of their minds and hearts, it only took one generation for the people of Israel to completely fall away from following the Lord. The Book of Judges tells this tragic story:

- **"After that generation** had been gathered to their fathers, another generation grew up, who knew neither the Lord nor what He had done for Israel" (Judges 2:10).
- **"Then the Israelites** did evil in the eyes of the Lord" (Judges 2:11).

Notice the order. First, God's people lost their spiritual memory (Judges 2:10). Then they fell into sin (Judges 2:11).

That's almost always the order. When a generation begins to lose its spiritual memory, when it's no longer awe-struck at how God saved them – it's the next generation that dies spiritually. That's what happened to the Israelites in the Book of Judges; that's what happened to the church in Sardis. That's why Jesus' word to them was: 'Remember.'

> "Remember what you have received and heard; obey it, and repent…"
> ~ Revelation 3:3

Remember. Obey. Repent.

Three commands, but notice the order. First is the call to *remember*. That's because waking up spiritually doesn't begin with doing a list of things for God. It begins with *remembering* what God has done for us. It's not about trying to white-knuckle our way to obedience. What we need most (and first) is to be reawakened to God's grace, so that we're inspired to live for Him out of gratitude for all that He's done for us. The church at Sardis needed to be reminded of all God had done for them in Christ, and *then* respond to that good news with obedience and repentance. That's what spiritually waking up looks like. It doesn't start with us *doing*. It starts with us *remembering*.

How Do I Remember?

For many of us, it's not enough just to be told *to* remember. We want to remember. The issue, usually, is how to jog our memories so we *can* remember all we've received and heard from Jesus – especially when we're so easily distracted by lesser things. So let me share some remembrance exercises that have been helpful to me staying close to what I've received and heard from Jesus. Maybe there will be an idea or two that you'll want to adopt.

1) Carrying a Nail

This is a very simple practice that I do from time to time that reminds me what Jesus did for me. I don't know about you, but my mind doesn't typically drift toward contemplating the cross throughout the day. I wish it did, but it doesn't. I need reminders. When I put my hand in my pocket to retrieve my keys or my wallet, and I feel the sharp end of a nail, it's this wonderful, tangible reminder of what Jesus did for me.

2) Journaling

Writing things down helps me to remember. Taking inventory of all I have to be grateful for sharpens my awareness of what I've received from God. And so every few weeks, my prayer journal entry is a remember exercise. Here's one from a few weeks ago:

"Heavenly Father, I have so much for which to give You thanks:
- *Forgiveness of my sins and new life in Christ*
- *The gift of Your Word, so that I can know You better*
- *Your Spirit in me – encouraging, correcting and guiding me*
- *A wife and children who love You*
- *A roof over our heads and food on our table*
- *Enough money to enjoy good things and share with others*
- *The privilege of being used of You to point others to Jesus*
- *The hope of Heaven to look forward to*

That's it. It took about five minutes to make that gratitude list. And then the prayer I wrote out after the remember exercise was this: *"Lord, I give You praise for all You've given me. Help me to live this day fully aware of all Your good gifts, full of gratitude for each one I've received."*

My spiritual memory gets jogged when I take five minutes to list what I've received from God.

3) Memorizing Scripture

Sometimes people get intimidated by this one, thinking you need a photographic memory to do it. You don't. The reality is we all memorize stuff all the time. Let me prove it to you:
- 2+2 = _____
- Roses are red, violets are _____
- Twinkle, twinkle, little _____

Whether it's math facts, poems, nursery rhymes, songs, movie quotes, sports statistics – we all memorize stuff. And contrary to what some people think, it doesn't take hours to memorize Scripture. Let me give you a window into how this has worked in my life.

Several years ago, I was finding myself getting anxious on Sunday mornings – so I decided to memorize a Scripture about God's peace – that I could go to when I got anxious. I chose Philippians 4:6-7: "Do not be anxious about anything. But in everything, by prayer and petition, with thanksgiving, present your requests to God. And the peace of God, which transcends all understanding, will guard your hearts and minds in Christ Jesus." I spent five minutes a day for a week on that verse – and then I had it memorized. Then on Sundays, when I felt myself drifting into anxiety, I would recite this verse – as a way of preaching to myself, as a way of *reminding* myself of this truth. I did this every Sunday for a few months, at which point I realized I had this verse hidden in my heart, to where I can recite it now whenever I find myself getting anxious.

Find a Scripture that reinforces some truth you're prone to forget, and then take five minutes a day for a week to memorize it. If you struggle to remember that God loves you, memorize Romans 5:8: "God demonstrates His own love for us in this: while we were still sinners, Christ died for us." If you tend to slip into people-pleasing, memorize Galatians 1:10: "Am I now trying to win the approval of human beings, or of God? Or am I trying to please people? If I were still trying to please people, I would not be a servant of Christ."

You see how this works. When there's something that you know you need to remember (about God or yourself), find a verse that reinforces that truth, take five minutes a day for a week to memorize it, and then begin preaching it to yourself. Before long, it will take root in your heart.

4) Strategically Placed Notes

This remembrance tool is based on Deuteronomy 6:8, where God says: "Tie these truths as symbols on your hands and bind them on your foreheads. Write them on the doorframes of your houses and on your gates." This sounds like an odd command, but God was so concerned that His people remember Him (and what He had done for them) that He had them hang reminders on themselves and their homes. Amanda and our daughters have taken the second part of this verse to heart. If you walk through our home, you'll find all sorts of strategically placed verses – on kitchen cupboards, bathroom mirrors, and bedroom walls.

Years ago, my youngest daughter, Glory, was struggling to understand God's forgiveness. She believed she needed to earn it. She tried hard to be the perfect little girl. Inside she was anxious and stressed out. I didn't know it at the time, but she eventually told me how she would make vows to God (before going to bed) that when she woke up, she would live that day sinless. Of course, all those vows did was lead Glory to despair, because she was keenly aware of how far short she fell of God's perfect standard (as we all do). And so she would go back and forth between making vows to be perfect, and despairing when she fell short.

When I finally picked up on what was happening in Glory's heart, I decided that on our next Daddy-Daughter date, we would get some hot chocolate, and look together at Romans 5:1, which says: "Since we have been justified through faith, we have peace with God through our Lord Jesus Christ." We talked about how peace with God doesn't come through being good enough for God to accept us. Peace comes through receiving "by faith" what God did to make us acceptable. By the grace of God, that was the light bulb moment for Glory. Romans 5:1 broke the spell of moralism, and opened her eyes to the good news of the gospel.

Right after that breakthrough, though, I remember Glory asking, 'But what if I forget?'

And so we went to the store to buy markers and paper, so she could write out this verse in bright, celebratory colors, and tape the words to her ceiling above her bed. It would be the first thing she read in the morning and the last thing she read at night. When she slipped back into thinking it was up to her to earn God's forgiveness, this verse jogged her memory, and helped her *remember* the truth of the gospel. Today, Glory is one of the most joy-filled young women I know. She is no longer trying to earn God's acceptance. She knows who and Whose she is; that she has been redeemed by the precious blood of Jesus; that she is now His beloved daughter. Glory now loves and serves Him – not out of guilt, but out of gratitude for what He's done for her.

Maybe there's a verse that you would do well to put on your ceiling, or your bathroom mirror, or the front screen of your phone or computer – somewhere to remind yourself of a truth that you know God wants you to stay close to.

5) The Lord's Supper

There is no more important remembrance exercise than communion, the meal that Christ instituted two thousand years ago, as a perpetual reminder of what He did for us. The bread is a symbol of Christ's body offered up for us on the cross. The juice is a symbol of His blood poured out for the forgiveness of our sins. "Do this in *remembrance* of Me," Jesus says.

Unfortunately, many Christians think communion can only be celebrated in a church building during a worship service. Not true. The first Lord's Supper took place in a home. That continued to be the pattern for the next three centuries. There's nothing in the Bible that says you can only celebrate communion in a church building, or that you need a pastor to serve you the elements. That's why from time to time, our family celebrates communion at home. Not because I'm a pastor, but because we're followers of Jesus, who need reminders of what He's done for us.

6) Re-reading impactful books

Reading great books by people who love Jesus is one of the ways God speaks to me. Unfortunately, I used to think if I read an impactful book, its insights would stay with me forever. But that's not what happens. After a few months (or weeks), the lessons from the book drift from my mind, and I forget them. Then I move on to the next new book, at which point I repeat the process all over again. That used to be my reading pattern.

Today, though, there are certain books I re-read every couple of years – in order to "remember what I received and heard" in them. I don't read as many new books as I used to, but that's okay. I've learned that it's important for me to read fewer new books so I have time to re-read books where God has already spoken to me. I'm reading now, for the fourth time, *The Cross of Christ,* by John Stott. It stirs up gratitude in me as I reflect on all that Jesus has done for me, which then inspires me to love and serve Him more. Perhaps there's a book you read years ago that impacted you. Go back and read it again, and be reminded of something you received and heard from God.

Two Things To Remember

I'm not surprised that *remember* is the word Jesus gave the church at Sardis to wake them up. It's the word He continues to use to wake me up, too, even after twenty years of ministry. Remembering all that God has done for me in Christ never gets old. My guess is that I'll be mining the depths of the gospel on into eternity. After all, if the gospel still occupies the attention of angels, whom Scripture says, "long to look into these things" (1 Pet 1:12), why should I ever tire of exploring its depths? The gospel should never get old! As David Prior says: "We never move on from the cross, only into a more profound understanding of the cross."[48]

JESUS' WORD TO THE CHURCH AT SARDIS: REMEMBER

As I get older, I'm sure I'll have my share of senior moments. No doubt I'll forget things of greater importance than what my wife asks me to bring her from the kitchen. But at the end of the day, my hope is that I can echo the words of John Newton, the ex-slave trader who was transformed by the gospel, who said: "Although my memory is fading, I remember two things very clearly: I am a great sinner, and Christ is a great Savior."

If those are the only two things I can remember, that will be enough.

Responding to Jesus' Letter

1) What word, phrase or image would you get tattooed onto your body (if you had to) – to help you remember something God wants you to stay close to?

   _____

2) If that feels too weird, simply spend a few minutes reflecting on the question: "What has God done for me (or taught me) that I need to remember?"

   a) Start out by reflecting on what He did for you 2,000 years ago – on the cross. That's the most important thing we need to stay close to.

   b) Then spend a few minutes thinking about other ways God has provided for you, or lessons He's taught you, or things He's spoken to you – that you know you would do well to stay close to. Write them down, and then thank God for all that you've received from Him.

3) Consider implementing one of the remembrance exercises mentioned: carrying a nail in your pocket, journaling, memorizing specific Scriptures, placing notes in strategic locations, celebrating communion, and re-reading impactful books.

Digging Deeper

1) Watch *The Gospel of John*, a full-length film that tells the story of Jesus, word for word, from the Fourth Gospel.

2) Read *Do Hard Things* (by Bret & Alex Harris) – an especially relevant book for a culture that has a tendency to slip into apathy and the path of least resistance.

3) Read *The Treasure Principle* (by Randy Alcorn) – a powerful little book about money, giving, and God's purpose for blessing us financially.

4) Purchase a communion set to have in your own home – to remember and celebrate what Jesus has done for us.

7

JESUS' WORD TO THE CHURCH AT PHILADELPHIA: PERSEVERANCE

ARE YOU GOING THROUGH A TOUGH TIME in life right now?

I'm not trying to depress you with that question, but I do want you to think about one area of your life where you're experiencing pain, hardship, disappointment or loss of some kind. You don't need to do anything about it right now. Just make a mental note.

One of the things you'll see in the letter to the church at Philadelphia is that the believers there were going through a very tough time. They faced some of the most brutal persecution of any of the churches in the Roman Empire. And yet, despite the hardship, they refused to give up or give in.

When I think about this church, I have in my mind the image of Beth Anne Deciantis finishing her race. Her life dream was to run a marathon in the Olympics. In order to qualify, though, she had to complete a 26-mile Olympic trial course in less than two hours forty-five minutes. *Runner's World* tells the story of her attempt:

> Beth started off the marathon strong, but she began having trouble around mile twenty-three.

> She pressed on through the pain of those next few miles, and eventually reached the final straight-away at two hours forty-three minutes, with just two minutes left to qualify. Two hundred yards from the finish line, though, Beth Anne stumbled and fell. Dazed, she stayed down on the ground for twenty seconds. The clock continued to tick: 2:44, less than a minute to go.
>
> Beth Anne staggered to her feet and began walking. Five yards short of the finish line, with ten seconds to go, she fell again. This time she began to *crawl*, with the crowd now cheering her on. Beth Anne crossed the finish line on her hands and knees. Her time? 2:44:57![49]

That's the image in my mind when I think about the believers in ancient Philadelphia: tired, weak, beat up, but determined not to give up. Persevering, pressing on, and giving everything they had to reach the finish line of their faith. It's no wonder Jesus sent them a letter. He did so, in part, to commend them for their faithful endurance. But He also wanted to give them a fresh reminder of Heaven — to encourage them to keep running the race that was marked out for them.

We need the same thing.

We, too, need to be reminded that there is another life beyond this one. We, too, need to be inspired by visions of the heavenly prize that awaits us, so that we're motivated to PERSEVERE through hardships in this life. We, too, need this letter from Jesus.

> "To the angel of the church in Philadelphia write: These are the words of him who is holy and true, who holds the key of David. What he opens no one can shut, and what he shuts no one can open. I know your deeds. See, I have placed before you an

JESUS' WORD TO THE CHURCH AT PHILADELPHIA: PERSEVERANCE

> open door that no one can shut. I know that you have little strength, yet you have kept my word and have not denied my name. I will make those who are of the synagogue of Satan, who claim to be Jews though they are not, but are liars—I will make them come and fall down at your feet and acknowledge that I have loved you. Since you have kept my command to endure patiently, I will also keep you from the hour of trial that is going to come on the whole world to test the inhabitants of the earth.
>
> I am coming soon. Hold on to what you have, so that no one will take your crown. The one who is victorious I will make a pillar in the temple of my God. Never again will they leave it. I will write on them the name of my God and the name of the city of my God, the new Jerusalem, which is coming down out of heaven from my God; and I will also write on them my new name. Whoever has ears, let them hear what the Spirit says to the churches."
>
> ~ Revelation 3:7-13

Historical Background

Because Christianity began as a movement within Judaism, most first century Jews and Christians attended synagogue together. Toward the end of the century, though, as the number of Christians grew, many of the synagogue leaders became uneasy about associating with them. They feared their exemption (to not worship Caesar) could be in jeopardy if they were too closely linked with those who called Jesus the King. After all, in the Roman Empire, there could only be one king: Caesar. So the synagogue leaders decided that the best way to preserve their exemption was to "close the door" (v7) of the synagogue on the Christians – to show Rome they were loyal to Caesar.

That is the context for Jesus introducing himself the way he does:

> "These are the words of him who is holy and true, who holds the key of David. What he opens no one can shut, and what he shuts no one can open. I know your deeds. See, I have placed before you an open door that no one can shut."
> ~ Revelation 3:7-8a

Jesus, the Master Communicator, intentionally uses "door" language at the beginning of the letter, because He wants His followers to know *He* is the door to God's Kingdom. The religious leaders may have closed the door of the *synagogue* on them, but Jesus has placed before them an open door to *God's Kingdom* that no one can shut.

This would have been incredibly encouraging to the Christians in Philadelphia, some of whom would have wondered if they were still part of God's people. After all, in the first century, to be kicked out of the synagogue was to be cut off from His people. Remember the blind man healed by Jesus in John 9? His parents were nervous to give Jesus the glory for the healing because they knew associating with Him would put them at risk of getting kicked out of the synagogue (John 9:22). That's the context for Jesus declaring, "I am the *Door*; whoever enters through me will be saved" (John 10:9). Jesus' point there is the same as in the letter to the church at Philadelphia. He wants His followers to know that even though the religious leaders have shut them out of the synagogue, they cannot be shut out of God's Kingdom. Jesus is the Open Door to the Kingdom!

Jesus' Word to the Church at Philadelphia: Perseverance

Never Give Up

The believers in Philadelphia may have lost the protection that came from being a member of the synagogue, but that didn't cause them to give up. They didn't play the victim card. They didn't wallow in self-pity. What little strength they had, they channeled into obedience. As Jesus says:

> "I know you have little strength, yet you have kept my word and have not denied my name."
> ~ Revelation 3:8b

The perseverance of these believers reminds me of David Rabin, a man who also had very little strength, but who made the most of it. John Ortberg tells his story:

> David Rabin was a professor of medicine at Vanderbilt University. While going through medical school, the disease that he found most frightening was… Lou Gehrig's Disease. David remembered being introduced to his first patient with this disease, and hearing the neurologist announce: "Hopeless! This man will be demeaned, isolated, unable to communicate, and probably dead in six months."
>
> When David Rabin turned 46, he himself was diagnosed with Lou Gehrig's Disease. And David knew what would happen to him: stiffness in the legs, then weakness; paralysis of the lower limbs and then the upper; eventually he would became trapped in a body that would no longer obey his commands. His tongue lost its ability to function; he could form words only with the greatest of difficulty, and eventually not at all. He lost his

ability to treat patients. He could no longer go to the hospital to work. He was on track to have a brilliant academic career; now he could no longer turn the pages of a book.

But there was one thing he would not surrender: *he would not surrender his spirit.* He heard from a fellow physician who also had LGD about a computer that could be operated by a single switch. That switch could be operated by anyone – however handicapped – if they retained the function of just one muscle group.

David had strength and ability in just one part of his body – his eyebrow muscle. And so for the next 4 years he used his eyebrow muscle.

With his eyebrow he could operate a computer. So with his eyebrow he learned to speak to his family, tell jokes to his friends, write papers, and review manuscripts. He carried on a medical consulting practice. He taught medical students. He published a comprehensive textbook on endocrinology and received a prestigious award for his work. And he did all this when the only thing he could control was his eyebrow. David Rabin said, "Sickness may challenge your body. But are you merely your body? Lameness may impede your legs. But you are not merely your legs. *Your will is bigger than your legs…*"

Here was a man whose body would not win any competitions or grace any magazine covers. It was twisted, seemingly useless, helpless, and hopeless. But it housed two assets: *an eyebrow muscle strong*

> *enough to twitch on command and a spirit that would not give up…* 50

Do you and I have a working eyebrow muscle?

Then we have no excuse for giving up on whatever God has called us to.

I'm inspired by people who refuse to give up, despite the deck being stacked against them. That's one of the reasons I'm thankful for opportunities to serve overseas, where I've gotten to see Christians persevering through all kinds of pain, poverty and persecution. Right now I'm teaching a Bible course to a group of Burundian students training to be pastors. They're actually teaching me; they're showing me what it looks like to follow in the footsteps of the church of Philadelphia, faithfully and joyfully serving Jesus, despite having so little.

I've seen this same spirit of perseverance in the church in the Middle East. Last year I had the privilege of visiting church leaders in Jordan, who are ministering to Iraqi believers who fled their homeland to escape ISIS. In the midst of unimaginable suffering, they are exemplifying the faith we in the West need to see – to shake us out of our complacency. Like the church in Philadelphia, these Iraqi Christians are using what little strength they have to remain faithful. Even Iraqi children kidnapped by ISIS are using their final breaths to declare their love for Jesus.

> Four Christian children in Iraq, under the age of 15, have been beheaded by ISIS, after they refused to renounce their Christian faith and become followers of Islam. A British reverend has spoken out about the atrocities suffered by Christians in Iraq, highlighting the shocking murder of the four youths, who dared to stand up to the jihadists. Canon Andrew White, known as the Vicar of Baghdad, recounted the horrific incident in an interview with the Orthodox Christian Network.

"Islamic State turned up and said to the children, 'You say the words that you will follow Mohammad.' The children, all under 15, four of them, said, "No, we love Yesua [Jesus]; we have always loved Yesua; we have always followed Yesua; Yesua has always been with us."

"They [ISIS] said, 'Say the words.' They [the children] said, 'No, we can't.' They chopped all their heads off. How do you respond to that? You just cry... That is what we have been going through and that is what we are going through," said the Canon, struggling to contain his emotions. 51

Jesus, forgive me for thinking that my life is difficult. Help me to learn from the persecuted church. Empower me to declare my faith in You, no matter the consequences.

True Vindication

Sharing our faith might cost us, but not like it cost the church in Philadelphia two thousand years ago, and not like it's costing the church in Iraq today. When I share my faith, about the worst that happens is I'm mocked or misunderstood. And yet sadly, when that happens, one of my first reactions is a desire for vindication. I want the people who are rejecting Jesus to know that I'm not crazy for believing in Him. The Christians in Philadelphia were probably craving vindication, too. They had been kicked out of the synagogue. They were social outcasts. They were viewed as fools. But Jesus did not counsel them to fight back or try to vindicate themselves. Jesus promised that He would vindicate them, and not in the way they were expecting it:

> "I will make them come and fall down at your feet and acknowledge that I have loved you."
> ~ Revelation 3:9b

JESUS' WORD TO THE CHURCH AT PHILADELPHIA: PERSEVERANCE

Notice Jesus does not say, "I will make them fall down at your feet and acknowledge that you were *right*, and they were *wrong*." Sadly, that's the kind of vindication I'm often looking for. I want people to know I'm right. Granted, right-ness is implied in Jesus' vindication, but that's not where the emphasis lies. Jesus says, "I will make them fall down at your feet and acknowledge that *I have loved you*."

There's a big difference between being vindicated because I'm *right*, and being vindicated because I'm *loved*. It's the difference between self-justification and justification by grace. It's the difference between self-righteousness and being made righteous by the cross of Christ, where "God proved His *love* for us" (Romans 5:8). Vindication is coming, not as a declaration of how *right* we are about God, but as a declaration of how *loved* we are by God.

If you're like me, and you wrestle with the desire to vindicate yourself on the basis of your 'right-ness,' here's a prayer I have in the margin of my Bible next to Revelation 3:9. It's a sixteen hundred year-old prayer that was frequently prayed by Saint Augustine:

> *"Lord, deliver me from the lust of always having to vindicate myself."*

If I really believe there is a day coming when Jesus will vindicate me, I won't need to defend myself whenever someone attacks me or my faith. I won't need to justify myself when I'm wronged. I won't need to play defense attorney for myself. Jesus is my Advocate (1 John 2:2). Therefore I can wait patiently for the day when He will vindicate me – not on the basis of my "right-ness" (self-righteousness) but on the basis of my "beloved-ness" (Christ-righteousness).

Jesus Will Keep Me _____ the Trial

Jesus continues to heap praise on the church at Philadelphia, commending them, in verse 10, for *keeping* His Word. In response, He promises to *keep* them:

> *"Since you have kept my commands to endure patiently, I will keep you from the hour of trial that is going to come upon the whole world."*
>
> ~ Revelation 3:10

This verse is one of the most hotly debated in all of Scripture. The argument about its meaning centers on the question of what exactly Jesus is promising. Is He promising to keep His church *from* the great tribulation described in the Book of Revelation? Some think so. For many interpreters, this verse is the centerpiece of an end-times eschatology that goes like this: *before things get too difficult here on earth, Jesus will come and rapture His church up to heaven – so we won't have to face it.*

Others don't think this is what Jesus is saying.

One of the reasons this verse gets debated is because the Greek phrase, "TEREO EK," can also be translated, "keep you *through*." Either translation is grammatically possible. This verse could read, "I will keep you *from* the hour of trial" or "I will keep you *through* the hour of trial." Because of the grammatical ambiguity, historical context is another tool for determining what this verse is saying. And on that point, Craig Keener cites the early church father, Polycarp, who noted that the persecution against the believers in Philadelphia actually *increased* in the years following this letter.52

In other words, Jesus did not keep them *from* trials. He kept them *through* trials.

This is the pattern throughout the New Testament. When Jesus prays for His disciples, he does not ask the Father to keep them physically safe. He prays that they might be kept spiritually safe from the evil one. He asks the Father to keep them *through* their trials: "My prayer is not that you take them out of the world but that you protect them from the evil one" (John 17:15).

The early church prayed this way, too. In Acts 4, after Peter and John were flogged and jailed for preaching Christ, the church gathered to pray. They didn't pray for physical protection from the oppressive rule of Rome. They didn't pray for a reprieve from the persecution of the Pharisees. They didn't pray for a new political leader who would give them religious freedom. Instead, they prayed for strength to keep preaching: "Now, Lord, consider their threats and enable your servants to speak Your word with great boldness" (Acts 4:29).

They prayed this way because this is how Jesus prayed for them – not to be kept safe *from* their trials, but to be kept strong *through* their trials. God answered their prayers, too, empowering them to preach boldly through their trials: "After they prayed, the place where they were meeting was shaken. And they were filled with the Holy Spirit and spoke the word of God boldly" (Acts 4:31).

According to church history, the legacy of the Apostles is one of God empowering them to faithfully preach Christ *through* their trials, even *unto death*.

- **Matthew** preached the gospel in Ethiopia, where he was ultimately martyred, executed with a halberd in the city of Nadabah in 60 AD.
- **Peter,** who believed himself unworthy of dying in the same way as his Lord, requested his Roman executioners crucify him upside down.
- **Thomas** preached in Parthia and India. The gospel was so offensive to his hearers that he was martyred by being thrust through with a spear.
- **James, the son of Zebedee,** was executed (according to Acts 12) with a sword, by order of King Herod Agrippa I.
- **James, the son of Alphaeus,** was stoned and clubbed to death.
- **Andrew** was dragged through the city of Patrae naked, thrown in prison, and then hanged upon a tree the next day, and stoned.
- **Philip** was scourged, imprisoned, and then crucified at Heliopolis, in Phrygia, in 54 AD.
- **Bartholomew,** who traveled to India to preach, and to give the people a copy of the Gospel of Matthew, was martyred there, beaten with rods and beheaded.

- **Thaddeus (Jude)** was crucified at Edessa in 72 AD.
- **Simon the Zealot** preached the gospel in Mauritania, Africa, and then in Britain, where, according to *Foxe's Book of Martyrs*, he was crucified in 74 AD.

The first followers of Jesus were not under the illusion that God's highest priority was to rescue them out of physical danger. They knew how Jesus had prayed for them (John 17). And that informed the way they prayed: for God's Spirit to empower them to preach the gospel even in the face of suffering and death (Acts 4).

This is how the persecuted Christians in the Middle East pray, how the persecuted Christians in Orissa, India pray, how the persecuted Christians in Sudan pray, and how the persecuted Christians in the underground church in China pray. Not for God to rescue them *from* their trials, but for God to give them courage to be bold witnesses for Christ *through* their trials, knowing that even their death will give way to a Paradise that God is preparing for those who love Him.

It's not wrong to ask God to rescue us from our trials. It's just not His highest priority. That's why, when trials come my way, I seek to respond like Meshach, Shadrach, and Abednego. In the face of King Nebuchadnezzar's demand that everyone in his kingdom bow down to a 90-foot idol or be thrown into a fiery furnace, Meshach, Shadrach, and Abednego respond:

> "O Nebuchadnezzar, we do not need to defend ourselves before you in this matter. If we are thrown into the blazing furnace, the God we serve is able to save us from it, and He will rescue us from your hand, O king. But even if He does not, we want you to know, O king that we will not serve your gods or worship the image of gold you have set up" (Daniel 3:16-18).

I love this story because of their faith that God was able to rescue them *from* the fiery furnace. God *can* deliver us *from* our trials. He's done so in my life on many occasions. That's why, when I'm in the middle of a trial, I typically begin by asking Him to rescue me *from* it. But this story reminds me, that even if God doesn't rescue me *from* my trial, He will strengthen me to go *through* it. Even if it leads to death – I can face it with courage and confidence that God has something better waiting for me in eternity.

Hold On: Something Better is Coming!

That's the promise Jesus makes toward the end of this letter, when He says:

> "I am coming soon. Hold on to what you have, so that no one will take your crown. To him who overcomes I will make a pillar in the temple of my God. Never again will he leave it. I will write on him the name of my God and the name of the city of my God, the New Jerusalem, which is coming down out of Heaven from my God."
> ~ Revelation 3:11-12

Jesus here is painting a picture of the glories of Heaven. The crown and the New Jerusalem are images of the coming Kingdom, where we'll enjoy restored fellowship with God and eternal life in a perfect paradise free of sin, suffering and death. And this promise is not just for the church at Philadelphia. It's for all of us who "hold on to what we've been given."

So what does it mean to "hold on"?

1) Don't Despair

If God chooses not to rescue me *from* whatever trial I'm facing, "holding on" means not buying into the enemy's lie that God has forgotten me. I've talked to so many people over the years who have been on the brink of bailing on Jesus because their life wasn't working out the way they thought it should. They thought following Jesus would make their lives easier; they thought God would rescue them *from* all of their trials. When He didn't, they started to believe God had abandoned them. Holding on means that no matter how difficult the circumstances of my life get, I will not despair. That doesn't mean I will never get discouraged. It just means that when I do, I will remind myself that Jesus never promised me a bed of roses on this side of Heaven. He never promised to rescue me *from* every trial. He promised to be with me *through* every trial.

2) Don't Give In To Self-Pity

Self-pity is the result of believing the lie that God is being too harsh with me. It's dangerous because it implies that I know (better than God) what will fulfill me. This is the same lie that Satan whispered back in the Garden of Eden. It's why Oswald Chambers said, "Self-pity is satanic." Self-pity leads to rationalization and moral compromise. Holding on means declaring: *The God I serve is able to save me from this trial. But even if He doesn't, then regardless of the pain, suffering or disappointment I might be feeling, I will not slip into self-pity, compromising what I know is right. I will walk in integrity no matter what – in my finances, in my work, in my relationships, in my entertainment, in everything.*

3) Trust God in the Uncertainty of the Immediate Future

Shadrach, Meshach, and Abednego didn't know how their story would turn out when they refused to bow down to that idol. They knew God *could* rescue them, but they didn't know if God *would* rescue them. The same is true for us. God is able to rescue us from our trials, but we don't always know if that will happen in this life. However, we do know our eternal future is certain. And because of that – we can trust God in the uncertainty of the here and now.

4) Keep the "End of the Story" Before You

When we put our trust in Jesus as Lord and Savior, we become heirs in His coming Kingdom. Our story, though presently marked by pain and disappointment, is now woven into His Story, a story marked by healing and restoration. Tragedy does not get the last word for those who are in Christ. Suffering does not get the last word for those who are in Christ. Death does not get the last word for those who are in Christ. 'Happily Ever After' is the last word for those who are in Christ. And that's not wishful thinking. It's based on the historical event of the resurrection, Jesus rising from the dead as proof and preview that He is the King, and His Kingdom is coming.

The more we keep our eyes fixed on this glorious coming Kingdom, the more motivated we'll be to endure through the hard part of our life. The reason some of us are tempted to give up or give in – is because Heaven seems so far away. 'Out of sight' becomes 'out of mind.' We're like the woman who tried to be the first person to swim from Catalina Island to the shore of California, who came up just short, because she couldn't see how close she was to her destination:

> In 1952, young Florence Chadwick stepped into the waters of the Pacific Ocean off Catalina Island, determined to swim to the shore of mainland California. She had already been the first woman to swim the English Channel both ways. The weather was foggy and chilly; she could hardly see the boats accompanying her. Still, she swam for fifteen hours. When she begged to be taken out of the water along the way, her mother, in a boat alongside her, told her she was close and that she could make it. But physically and emotionally exhausted, she decided to stop swimming and get pulled out of the water. It wasn't until she was on the boat that she discovered the shore was less than half a mile away. At a news conference the

next day she said, "While I was swimming – all I could see was the fog.... *I think if I could have seen the shore, I would have made it."* 53

One of the reasons Jesus paints a picture of Heaven, and tells us to "hold on," is so we don't let the fog of this world blur our vision of how close we are to the finish line of our faith. Jesus doesn't want us to give up or give in (in any area of life) before we get there. This is why, at the beginning of the chapter, I invited you to make a mental note of that area of life where you're experiencing hardship or disappointment. That's the place you most need to keep the End of the Story in view.

So let me ask you again: Where in life are you going through something difficult, for which you need to keep the End of the Story in your mind, so that you're inspired to hold on and persevere?

- Maybe you're facing something at home or work that's so discouraging – you feel like throwing in the towel. Deep down, though, you know it's an assignment for which Jesus is saying, "Don't give up. Hold on. Persevere."
- Maybe there's a relationship challenge you're facing right now. Maybe you're struggling with a spouse or a child or a parent or a friend. Maybe you feel like giving up on this relationship. But deep down, you know Jesus is saying, "Don't bail. Hold on. Persevere."
- Maybe you're struggling with an addiction or habit or pattern that is sabotaging your life. You've surrendered it to Jesus, but you're not yet totally free from its grip. The temptation, at times, is still so strong, you just want to give in and indulge in that thing you know will bring a little short-term relief. But when you get quiet before Jesus, you can hear Him whispering, "Don't go back there. Hold on. Persevere."
- Maybe you're discouraged about all of life. Some mornings you want to stay in bed and not even face the day. You believe in Jesus and you know Heaven is your destination.

JESUS' WORD TO THE CHURCH AT PHILADELPHIA: PERSEVERANCE

But right now, His coming Kingdom seems irrelevant and far away. Maybe you need to ask God to open your eyes to see a glimpse of the End of the Story, and open your ears to hear Him say: "Don't give up. Hold on. In the end, persevering will be worth it."

Jesus knows all about the pain and hardship of your life. He knows all about what you've lost, and what you've had to endure. He knows all about the relational disappointment, the financial strain, the physical pain, and the unrealized dreams. But He also knows that the glorious future He's preparing for you will make your present suffering pale in comparison. As Mother Teresa famously said, "In light of heaven, the worst suffering on earth, a life full of the most atrocious tortures on earth, will be seen to be no more serious than one bad night in a cheap hotel."

Jesus *can* give that perspective to you.
Jesus *wants* to give that perspective to you.
Jesus *will* give that perspective to you – if you ask Him for it.

Responding to Jesus' Letter

1) Take a moment now to write down that area in life where you most need to hear Jesus say those words: "I am coming soon. Hold on. Don't give up."

   _____

2) Proclaim the truth of God's glorious future over yourself and over that area of your life that is hard. Allow Jesus to work His Word into your mind and heart.

   > "Therefore we do not lose heart. Though outwardly we are wasting away, yet inwardly we are being renewed day by day. For our light and momentary troubles **(Insert that area of life where you are tempted to give up or despair)** are achieving for us an eternal glory that far outweighs them all. So we fix our eyes not on what is seen, but on what is unseen, since what is seen is temporary, but what is unseen is eternal" (2 Cor 4:16-18).

3) There's nothing wrong with asking God to deliver you from your trials. Those prayers are found throughout the Bible, too. It's even okay to start there. But don't get stuck there. If you've already prayed for God to rescue you *from* the trial – maybe now it's time to pray for God to give you the eternal perspective and power to persevere *through* the trial. Pray for a fresh vision of the End of the Story – so that you're inspired to hold on and press on *through* whatever trial you're facing.

4) Utilize the 'Digging Deeper' next steps to allow God to transform your mind so that you see the hard parts of your life through the lens of Heaven.

JESUS' WORD TO THE CHURCH AT PHILADELPHIA: PERSEVERANCE

Digging Deeper

1) Read *Heaven* (by Randy Alcorn), the most impactful book I've ever read for helping me to understand all that Jesus is preparing for me, and all that He is preparing me for.

2) Read *Epic* (by John Eldredge), and train yourself to see your life, especially the hard parts, in light of the epic story of the Gospel, and the Happily Ever After that is coming.

3) Read *Jesus Freaks* (Voice of the Martyrs), and be inspired and challenged by stories of Christians who have not only lived for Jesus, but who have been willing to die for Him.

4) Watch your favorite fairy tale or epic movie, especially noting the pain and hardship that marks the middle part of the story. After it's over, ask yourself if Jesus, the One who died for you, won't come up with an even more inspiring ending to your story?

5) Utilize www.epm.org (Eternal Perspective Ministries), a fantastic ministry site, full of resources that will help you keep your eyes on Heaven, so you're inspired to persevere.

8

JESUS' WORD TO THE CHURCH AT LAODICEA: HUMILITY

Imagine a ship without a captain.
Imagine a class without a teacher.
Imagine a courtroom without a judge.
Imagine a football team without a quarterback.
Imagine trying to play 'Follow the Leader' without a leader.

It doesn't work.

AND YET THIS IS HOW THE BELIEVERS IN THE church at Laodicea were living: like they no longer needed their Leader, Jesus. They still gathered together for church. They still believed in Jesus. They just weren't dependent on His leadership. They weren't desperate for His help. They didn't think they needed His wisdom or guidance. But Jesus knew better. So He sent them a letter to confront their pride and independence, and call them to HUMILITY:

> "To the angel of the church in Laodicea write: These are the words of the Amen, the faithful and true witness, the ruler of God's creation. I know your deeds, that you

are neither cold nor hot. I wish you were either one or the other! So, because you are lukewarm—neither hot nor cold—I am about to spit you out of my mouth. You say, 'I am rich; I have acquired wealth and do not need a thing.' But you do not realize that you are wretched, pitiful, poor, blind and naked. I counsel you to buy from me gold refined in the fire, so you can become rich; and white clothes to wear, so you can cover your shameful nakedness; and salve to put on your eyes, so you can see.

Those whom I love I rebuke and discipline. So be earnest and repent. Here I am! I stand at the door and knock. If anyone hears my voice and opens the door, I will come in and eat with that person, and they with me.

To the one who is victorious, I will give the right to sit with me on my throne, just as I was victorious and sat down with my Father on his throne. Whoever has ears, let them hear what the Spirit says to the churches."
~ Revelation 3:14-22

You may have noticed that there are no words of affirmation in this letter, which is unusual. With the exception of His letter to the church at Sardis, Jesus always has something in every church that He can affirm. But there are no words of commendation for the Laodiceans. Jesus cuts right to the chase, telling them they have become so spiritually lukewarm that He's about to *"vomit"* them out of his mouth (v16).

How's that for a greeting?

Some translations say, "I am about to *spit* you out of my mouth," but that is a very soft, sanitized translation of the Greek.

The word is literally "vomit." Translating it 'spit' just goes to show that some translators aren't sure what to do with this image of Jesus, the Son of God… *vomiting*.

I get that. I mean, think of all the inspirational paintings of Jesus you've ever seen, where He's carrying a lamb on his shoulders, or opening the eyes of the blind, or feeding the hungry, or giving his life on the cross. But have you ever seen a painting of Jesus vomiting? I haven't. Jesus and *vomit* don't seem to go together. And that's the point. Jesus uses this disturbing, grotesque image – to get the attention of a church that's become spiritually lukewarm.

To understand how the church got here (and why Jesus warns them that He is about to vomit them out of His mouth) requires some historical background.

Historical Context

Laodicea was a wealthy, educated, sophisticated city. Relative to the rest of the Roman Empire, they had it all. And they took great pride in their abundance. According to Darrell Johnson, the motto of Laodicea was: *"We have need of nothing."*[54]

In other words, that's what you would have seen on the billboard as you rolled into the city: "Welcome to Laodicea: we have need of nothing!"

The city of Laodicea was so proud of their self-sufficiency that in 60 A.D., after a massive earthquake destroyed their city and several other cities in their province, the emperor offered federal aid to help these cities rebuild. And everyone took it, *except Laodicea*. Can you imagine that? This would have been like New Orleans, after Hurricane Katrina, refusing the federal disaster funds offered to them by the United States government! Can you imagine? That's what Laodicea did. They told Rome they didn't *need* their help.[55]

'Welcome to Laodicea: We have need of *nothing*!'

The city of Laodicea was the Wall Street of the first century. They were a banking powerhouse, the financial center of the

Roman Empire. Earlier in the first century, the Jews in Jerusalem were facing a famine, and so appealed to their fellow Jews in Laodicea for help. A collection was taken up, and over twenty-two pounds of gold (over $500,000 in today's currency) was raised.[56]

'Welcome to Laodicea: We have need of *nothing*!'

Laodicea was also the world's leader in the production of textiles and clothing. They were the Paris of the first century, the fashion runway of the Empire. They had the reputation of being the best-dressed people in the entire province of Asia.

'Welcome to Laodicea: We have need of *nothing*!'

Laodicea was also setting the pace for entertainment in the Roman Empire. They were the Hollywood and Vegas of the first century. They had their own theater for plays, and even their own stadium for sporting events.

'Welcome to Laodicea: We have need of *nothing*!'

Laodicea was also famous for its medicine, especially optometry. They had an eye clinic, which had developed a salve ointment that was proving effective in healing weak eyesight. They were the scientific hub of the Empire, sort of a Johns Hopkins of the first century.

'Welcome to Laodicea: We have need of *nothing*!'

Imagine a city with the financial capital of New York, the fashion prestige of Paris, the glitz and glamour of Vegas and Hollywood, and the medical technology of Johns Hopkins. No wonder the city of Laodicea boasted about how they had it all.

But what does that have to do with the church at Laodicea?

Evidently, the same spirit of self-sufficiency that marked the *city* of Laodicea had infiltrated the *church* in Laodicea. Jesus, speaking to His *church,* in v17, says: "You say, 'I am rich; I have acquired wealth and do not need a thing.'" That sounds just like the motto of the city of Laodicea. In other words, instead of the church influencing the culture to see their need for Jesus, the culture had influenced the church, blinding them from seeing their need for Jesus.

From the world's perspective, Laodicea seemed to have it all. But the truth is – they didn't. They were lacking something very

JESUS' WORD TO THE CHURCH AT LAODICEA: HUMILITY

important: *their own local water source.* For all of their wealth and ingenuity, the citizens of Laodicea did not have access to even one drop of hot or cold water. And that was a point for which the proud people of Laodicea did not like to be reminded, especially since all of the other great cities of the Empire had their own hot and cold water.

Just six miles down the road was Hierapolis, a city famous for its hot springs, which produced water that could be used for baths, right out of the tap. The water was hot enough to be used for medicinal purposes, too, and even for making special drinks, sort of a first century Starbucks. Ten miles in the other direction was Colossae, a city famous for its mountain fresh cold water, the kind used for providing a refreshing drink on a hot day.

All of the major, modern cities of the Roman Empire had hot water, cold water, or both. But Laodicea had neither. And this was a major blow to their pride. After all, how great can your city be if you don't even have your own water?

So what did they do?

With their vast wealth, the city of Laodicea built an aqueduct, with miles of pipes, so that they could bring in hot and cold water from Hierapolis and Colossae. It was a costly engineering feat. But it didn't solve their problem. By the time the water from these cities made its way into Laodicea, the cold water from Colossae was no longer cold, and the hot water from Hierapolis was no longer hot. Both became *lukewarm* on the journey to Laodicea, such that the water was neither hot enough for baths nor cold enough for drinking. In fact, the taste of the water, by the time it reached Laodicea, was so bad, so lukewarm, that unsuspecting tourists would drink it – and frequently end up – are you ready? *Vomiting!*

The great city of Laodicea, with its entrepreneurial spirit, couldn't do anything about their water problem. And so Jesus, the Master Communicator, puts His finger on this one aspect of life His people knew they couldn't fix, in order to pull the rug out from under their pride and self-sufficiency. This was Jesus' way of saying: *You may have a strong economy, you may have your own clothing industry, and you may have your own medical center. But as you well know, your water, which is the source of life, makes people who visit you and drink it, vomit. And that's my response, too, when I visit your church and drink in your lukewarm, self-sufficient spirituality.*

Let me clarify a couple of things about self-sufficiency: taking responsibility to provide for ourselves is a good thing. There's nothing noble about letting someone else pay our bills. That's why Paul says: "If you don't work, you don't eat" (2 Thess 3:10). Jesus is not rebuking the Laodiceans for working hard, making money or taking responsibility for themselves. He's not even taking issue with their medical technology, fashion or entertainment. There's nothing necessarily wrong with any of these. What Jesus is calling out is His people allowing themselves to be seduced by a spirit of self-sufficiency, where they no longer think they need His wisdom and help – because they've pretty well figured out how to do life without Him.

For many in the West (even in the church), this is how we live, too. We believe in Jesus. But Jesus is not someone we think we need to depend upon on a daily basis. We've got our own resources for that: money, medicine, technology, entertainment, etc. We say we depend upon Jesus, but these are the things we often turn to for security, guidance, or comfort.

We're not that different from those in Laodicea.

Self-Delusion

Laodicea's pride deluded them into thinking of themselves (and their ingenuity) more highly than they ought to have. But let's not be too hard on them. The Christians of Laodicea didn't have the monopoly on self-delusion. We all have blind spots. John Ortberg writes about what psychologists call a massive integrity blind spot in human nature called the *self-serving bias.*

In one survey, 800,000 high school students were asked whether they were above or below average in social skills. Statistically, there should be a 50-50 split. Half the students should consider themselves 'above average' and half the students should consider themselves 'below average.' Can you guess what percentage of students rated themselves as being above average? More than 99%. And 25% of those students rated themselves in the top 1%!

This self-serving bias isn't just found in teen-agers. It's prevalent in adults, too. Another study surveyed people who were in hospitals, recovering from car accidents, serious accidents which they admitted were their fault. Ironically, more than half of these people, *who had just caused a car accident*, still rated themselves as being a better driver than the majority of their peers.

You might think that being educated would dramatically decrease this self-serving bias. Nope. The percentage of college professors who rated themselves as being above average – compared to their fellow professors? 88%.

The church isn't exempt from this self-serving bias, either. George Barna surveyed pastors, those who are called to embody humility and maintain a right view of themselves. They were asked to rate their preaching in comparison to their colleagues. 90% of the pastors considered themselves to be better preachers than their peers.

So much for the theory that our society has a self-esteem problem!

Ortberg concludes his summary of the self-serving bias study by saying: "And perhaps most ironic of all: when people have the concept of the self-serving bias carefully explained to them, the majority of those people rate themselves as above average in their ability to handle the self-serving bias!"[57]

The church at Laodicea had fallen prey to the self-serving bias. Their city's self-proclaimed greatness had crept into their thinking, influencing them to live as if they didn't really need Jesus in their daily lives. They certainly would have called themselves Christians. But they didn't see their desperate need to invite Jesus into their everyday lives, not when they already had life pretty well figured out.

Laodicea's pride and self-proclaimed greatness, reminds me of Muhammad Ali, the famous heavyweight boxing champion, who often proclaimed, "I am the Greatest!" In the ring, Muhammad Ali arguably was the greatest boxer of all time. But Ali's arrogance spilled over into situations where he would have done well to admit his need. There's a story of Ali refusing to fasten his seatbelt on an airplane flight. Repeatedly, the flight attendants requested that he sit down and put on his seatbelt, to which Ali kept saying, "Superman don't need no seatbelt; Superman don't need no seatbelt!" Finally, one of the flight attendants brought Ali back down to earth by giving him a strong dose of reality: "Honey, Superman don't need no airplane, either... so why don't you sit down and buckle up!"

The Church at Laodicea acted as if they were Superman. They thought they were so great, they no longer needed Jesus. The motto of the city had become the attitude of the church: 'We have need of nothing!'

Spiritual Diagnosis

This is why the Great Physician, Jesus, confronts their pride and their self-sufficiency by giving them a diagnosis of their true spiritual condition.

> "You say, 'I am rich; I have acquired wealth and do not need a thing.' But you do not realize that you are wretched, pitiful, poor, blind and naked."
>
> ~ Revelation 3:17

How's that for a diagnosis? And there's no need for a second opinion. Jesus, with spiritual X-ray vision, sees through all of the outward markers of success to their true condition: *You think you've got it all together,* Jesus says, *but actually you're wretched, pitiful, poor, blind, and naked.*

And given that diagnosis, here is what Jesus prescribes:

> "I counsel you to buy from me gold refined in the fire, so you can become rich; and white clothes to wear, so you can cover your

shameful nakedness; and salve to put on your eyes, so you can see."
~ Revelation 3:18

What Jesus does here is brilliant. He brings up the very things the Laodiceans took pride in: money, clothing, and medical care. And then, one at a time, He shows them how spiritually empty they still are, even with them.

The believers in Laodicea took pride in their money. They had a lot of it. But Jesus says, 'You're actually **poor**.' He says, *You may have a lot of money in the bank, but you're broke when it comes to the things of My Kingdom. So here's my advice: buy from Me lasting treasure, the kind that's been refined in the fire, and then you'll have wealth that will last for eternity.*

The believers in Laodicea took pride in how they clothed themselves. They looked good. But Jesus says, 'You're actually **naked**.' He says, *The world may be impressed with your fine wardrobe, but before Me, you're exposed, unable to withstand the bright light of my holiness. So here's my advice: buy from Me white clothes to wear, so you can cover your shameful nakedness.*

The believers in Laodicea took pride in their medical capability to heal weak eyesight. They had a world class eye clinic. But Jesus says, 'You're actually **blind**.' He says, *You may be able to do Lasix surgery for your physical eyes, but spiritually, you're blind as a bat. So here's my advice: buy from Me the salve that can be applied to the spiritual eyes of your heart, so you can truly see.*

Are you catching the irony of Jesus' counsel? "I advise you to *buy* from Me," he says. Jesus intentionally uses financial language because He knows it will grab the attention of the business-minded Laodiceans. But there's a twist to his financial advice. Jesus counsels them to "purchase" things that money can't buy.

Grace > Money

The eternal treasure that Jesus is talking about can't be found on Amazon.com. The clothing that wraps us in the love and acceptance of God can't be found at Nordstrom. The ointment that opens the spiritual eyes of our hearts can't be found at Walgreens. In other words, we don't have the means to get for ourselves what we most need. Only God's grace has that kind of purchasing power. And the only way to procure God's grace is to recognize that we need it – because in God's economy, *spiritual poverty* is the path to riches: "Blessed are the poor in spirit, for theirs is the Kingdom of Heaven" (Matthew 5:3).

The church at Laodicea needed to swallow their pride and admit they *needed* something from Jesus they couldn't get for themselves. And that meant relinquishing their self-sufficiency, and letting Jesus into those places in their lives where He wanted to come in. That's the remedy for a spirit of self-sufficiency: letting Jesus in, which is what He invites them to do next:

> "Be earnest, and repent. Here I am! I stand at the door and knock. If anyone hears my voice and opens the door, I will come in and eat with him, and he with me."
> ~ Revelation 3:19-20

When we finally take a posture of humility before God, and repent, admitting our need for Jesus, we don't have to go any farther than the front door of our heart to let Him in. That's where He's been standing the whole time, knocking, waiting for us.

The Door Can Only Be Opened From the Inside

Jesus won't break down the door. He won't hi-jack our free will. He won't barge in, because there's no handle on the outside of this door. It can only be opened from the inside, by us. Of course, let's not give ourselves credit for opening the door. That's the very self-centered, self-sufficient spirit Jesus is confronting in this letter! Yes, it's our choice to let Jesus in, but He is the Initiator in the relationship. Our decision to let Him in is always preceded by His grace to pursue us. As Jesus says: "No one can come to me unless the Father who sent me draws them" (John 6:44). So while I might be the one who opens the front door, it's God who sets a fire in my basement (where I'm hiding or avoiding Him) to get me to run upstairs and open it!

God is sovereign. At the same time, God also honors our free will – even when it means allowing us to reject Him over and over, leaving Him standing at the door, knocking, waiting for us to let Him in. Think about that. The Creator of the universe takes a posture of vulnerability, reaching for relationship with us, even after we've ignored His knocking. Why would He do that? Why would He even want to come in after we've rejected Him?

Why Does Jesus Want to Come in?

Some people think it's only so that He can give us a spiritual spanking for all of the times we've blown it or sinned against Him. Others think it's because He wants to keep us from having too much fun. But neither is true. Jesus wants to come in, so He can cleanse us from our guilt, heal us of our shame, give us His peace, and empower us to live a new life. Jesus wants to come in and dwell with us, so that He can show us how to live the life He created us to live – in an ongoing relationship with Him. That's what Jesus is offering when He says, "I will come in and eat with you."

In the ancient Middle Eastern world, sharing a meal was about establishing friendship and covenant with one another. It was a way of saying, *I want to have a relationship with you, where I share with you all that I am, and you share with me all that you are.*

So when Jesus offers to come in and share a meal with the Laodiceans (or with us), it's His way of saying, *No matter how many times you've rebelled against Me, no matter how often you've shut me out of your life, or chosen to live life on your own terms – I still want a relationship with you, where I share with you all that I am, and you share with Me all that you are.*

We definitely get the better end of the covenant – since what we bring to the table is our sin, and what He brings to the table is forgiveness, eternal life, and a thousand more blessings beside.

This is why Martin Luther refers to it as "the sweetest exchange." And the only thing separating us from this offer of covenant with the God of the universe – is the door of our heart, where Jesus is knocking, waiting for us to surrender our pride and let Him in.

Laodicea in Me

Sadly, it's possible to be part of a church and never take this step. Like the church in Laodicea, in America we've created a religion where many of us call ourselves Christians, and yet we're spiritually blind, pitiful and wretched – because in our pride, we refuse to acknowledge our *need* for Jesus to save us from our sins, and our *need* for Jesus to come in and take charge of our lives.

We want to be in charge. We think we can run our life better than He can.

Most of us aren't so bold as to say we don't want Jesus in our lives *at all*. We just want Jesus to take the seat next to us – as our co-pilot. Maybe you've seen that bumper sticker that says, "Jesus is my co-pilot!" Personally, I like the one that reads: "If Jesus is your co-pilot, switch seats."

Some of us want Jesus to be our Savior, but not our Lord.

That's what those of us who have received Christ's forgiveness are saying when we refuse to let Him take charge of our lives. We're saying, "Jesus, thanks for going to the cross and paying the price to save me from my sins, so I can look forward to Heaven, instead of Hell. But I'll take it from here. I don't want you messing up my life."

It's that kind of proud, luke-warm, self-sufficient attitude that makes Jesus want to puke. Jesus is not looking to be your co-pilot. He's not looking to be your butler, or your administrative assistant. Jesus has His own specially designed plans for you and your life, which is why He doesn't just want to come through the front door of the house, and sit on your couch. He wants access to every room in your house. C.S. Lewis explains why:

> Imagine yourself as a living house. God comes in to rebuild that house. At first, perhaps, you can understand what He is doing. He is getting the drains right and stopping the leaks in the roof and so on; you knew that those jobs needed doing and so you are not surprised. But presently He starts knocking the house about in a way that hurts abominably and does not seem to make any sense. What on earth is He up to? The explanation is that He is building quite a different house from the one you thought of–throwing out a new wing here, putting on an extra floor there, running up towers, making courtyards. You thought you were being made into a decent little cottage: but He is building a palace. He intends to come and live in it Himself.[58]

Jesus is not content to tweak your life a little here and there. He wants to transform you.

The question is: Will you let Him in so that He can do what He wants to do? Not just let Him in through the front door of the house, long enough to pronounce your sins forgiven – while you lock all the rooms that you don't want Him disturbing. Will you let Him in the front door – and then allow Him to take charge of the whole house?

I still remember the day I humbled myself, and opened the *front door* of my heart, letting Jesus come in and save me from my sins, and fill me with His peace and the assurance of Heaven. That was (and still is) the most important door I've ever opened. I've never regretted it. But Jesus wasn't content to just be my Savior. He was not content to step into the narthex of the home, forgive my sins, wish me well, and then head out to leave me in charge of the house. He came to live with me. His endgame is to transform me. And so, Jesus began knocking on the other doors of the house, seeking to come into those rooms and transform every area of my life.

- It was a few months later when I let Jesus into the room: *My Entertainment World.*
- It was a year later when I let Jesus into the room: *My Fears.*
- And another year later when I let Jesus into the room: *My Finances.*
- And then sometime soon thereafter when I let Jesus into the room: *My Future.*
- There are some rooms I invite Him into daily, like the room: *My Work.*

And so on…

At least for me, I have to be intentional to open up the doors to these rooms. I don't naturally drift toward surrender in any area of my life. My default is to take charge and stay in control. That's why I need to make a conscious decision of my will to humble myself and let Jesus come into each of these rooms. And it's not usually a one-time surrender. I've needed to let Jesus come in and take charge of some areas of my life more than once, because I'm so prone to taking back the reins. But every time I respond to His knocking and let Him in, He does what He promises: He brings His healing and help, and increases my sense of His presence in my life.

It's not easy to admit, but I've struggled with pride and self-sufficiency for most of my life. I'm not where I was 27 years ago when I first surrendered my life to Jesus. I've grown. But there are still days when I find myself tempted to drink the lukewarm water of Laodicea, the kind with the label on it, which reads: "I have need of nothing. I've got everything under control."

One of the things God continues to remind me of is that *humility* is the antidote to pride; that *humility* is the way to combat this spirit of self-sufficiency. I'm not talking about false humility, where I try to make myself sound worse than I am. I'm talking about honestly assessing whether Jesus is really in charge of every area of my life, and then being willing to repent of those places where I am still doing things in my own strength, like the believers in Laodicea. It's such a simple concept, but one of the significant lessons God has been teaching me is from James 4:6, where it says: "God opposes the proud, but gives grace to the humble."

Whenever I find myself drifting toward independence or self-sufficiency, I'm reminded of this Scripture. And it moves me to exchange my pride for a spirit of humility, where I pray a very simple prayer, *"God, even though I'm tempted to think I'm smart enough or hard-working enough to handle this on my own, I know I need You to enter this room of my life and take charge."* And whenever I'm willing to pray that prayer and take that step, I really do experience what Jesus promises. Don't get me wrong – sometimes letting Jesus in means allowing Him to make changes in my life that might be painful. But with Jesus, even the pain is marked by peace. Even the pain is marked by a deep conviction that He is transforming me into the person He created me to be. It's what He does – if we'll humble ourselves and let Him in.

Take Down the 'Do Not Disturb' Sign

So is there a room in your house where you've posted a 'Do not Disturb' sign? Get honest. Maybe there's a room in your life where you don't want Jesus messing around. Maybe you're ashamed of what's in there. Maybe you're afraid of what'll happen if Jesus goes in there. Or maybe you're just lazy, and you don't want to deal with what's in there. Or maybe you've worked hard to make that room like it is, and if Jesus goes in there, He might have other plans for it. Or maybe that room is a mess, but it's your mess; you like it the way it is. You don't want any help from anyone for that room – not even Jesus. Perhaps today, though, you know it's time to let Jesus in. You know it's time to let Jesus come in and do whatever He wants to that room: clean it up, remodel it – do whatever He needs to do to make that room fit for the King of glory!

Responding to Jesus' Letter

My guess, if you're still reading this book, is that you've already invited Jesus to come into your life. But just in case you haven't, let me encourage you to take that step right now. Jesus is standing at the front door of your heart, seeking to come in and save you, cleanse you of all your sin and give you the assurance of eternal life. Maybe today is the day you swallow your pride, acknowledge your need for a Savior, and receive the forgiveness that Jesus died on the cross to provide. If you'll humble yourself, give Him your sin, and put your trust in His finished work on the cross, He will do that for you, right at this very moment!

Or maybe you've already received Christ's forgiveness. You've let Him in the front door of your heart. But if you're honest, there are other rooms in your life that you've not yet let Him into. The question for you is: "Will you let Him in?"

Will you let Him into:

- The room called, "My Finances"
- The room called, "My Future"
- The room called, "My Work"
- The room called, "My Family"
- The room called, "My Past"
- The room called, "My Marriage"
- The room called, "My Parenting"
- The room called, "My Health Concerns"
- The room called, "My Relational Disappointments"
- The room called, "My Entertainment"
- The room called, "My Sexuality"
- The room called, "My Fears"
- The room called, "My Failures"
- The room called, "My Dreams"
- The room called, "My Secrets"

JESUS' WORD TO THE CHURCH AT LAODICEA: HUMILITY

1) Let today be the day you look back on, and say, "That's the day I let Jesus into the room, called: 'My _____, and He began transforming that area of my life.'"

2) Write down in the margin of your Bible (next to Revelation 3:20) today's date, and the specific room of your life you're inviting Jesus into.

Digging Deeper

1) Read *Radical* (by David Platt), a great prophetic word to the American church about what it looks like to follow Jesus in the context of a culture that is a lot like Laodicea.

2) Take five minutes to listen to the hymn, *Take My Life* – and prayerfully consider if there are any other rooms in your life where you need to let Jesus in.

9

JESUS IN ME > ME TRYING HARDER

NO MATTER HOW HARD WE TRY, WE cannot perfectly live out what Jesus calls us to in these seven letters. Not in our own strength. We don't have it in us. But Jesus does. And the good news is: He *is* in us!

When we put our trust in Jesus to save us, He comes to dwell within us – just as He promised the church at Laodicea, and just as is proclaimed throughout the New Testament. As the Apostle Paul declares, "I no longer live, but Christ lives in me" (Galatians 2:20).

This is where our true power lies: Jesus in us!

I cannot live out the kind of love I'm called to, but **JESUS IS LOVE**, and Jesus is in me.

> "Having loved his own who were in the world, He now showed them the full extent of His love... He got up from the meal, took off His outer clothing, and wrapped a towel around His waist. After that, He poured water into a basin and began to wash His disciples' feet."
> ~ John 13:1,5

Jesus demonstrated His love by washing the feet of sinners like Peter (who would deny him), Judas (who would betray him), and the other disciples (who would desert him). Jesus showed the even greater depths of His love by going to the cross for sinners like you and me. Jesus is love. And Jesus is in me. Therefore, Jesus can live out His love through me.

I cannot live out the courage I'm called to, but **JESUS IS COURAGEOUS**, and Jesus is in me.

> "In this world you will have trouble. But take heart! I have overcome the world."
> ~ John 16:33

Jesus had the courage to stand up against the religious and political leadership, unintimidated by their strong-arm tactics, and refusing to flinch in the face of their threats. Jesus looked down the barrel of Death itself, courageously dying, in order to defeat the grave. Jesus is courageous. And Jesus is in me. Therefore, Jesus can live out His courage through me.

I cannot live out the purity I'm called to, but **JESUS IS PURE**, and Jesus is in me.

> "Behold the Lamb of God, who takes away the sin of the world!"
> ~ John 1:29

Jesus never compromised. Not when Satan was tempting Him in the Wilderness after 40 days of fasting. Not in Gethsemane, when He was sweating drops of blood, asking the Father if there was any other way besides the cross to redeem us. Jesus refused to take shortcuts. Jesus is pure. And Jesus is in me. Therefore, Jesus can live out His purity through me.

I cannot live out the repentance I'm called to, but **JESUS REPENTED**, and Jesus is in me.

> "Then Jesus came from Galilee to the Jordan to be baptized by John. But John tried to

deter him, saying, 'I need to be baptized by you, and do you come to me?' Jesus replied, 'Let it be so now; it is proper for us to do this to fulfill all righteousness.'"
~ Matthew 3:13-15

Jesus did not need to repent. He was sinless. But He submitted to John's baptism of repentance to identify with us in our sins. He was repenting *for* us – so that His righteousness could be shared *with* us. His repentance was not simply an *example* for us to follow. Jesus *is* our repentance, who "fulfilled all righteousness" – so that we could be righteous before God. Jesus repented for me. And Jesus is in me. Therefore, Jesus can live out His repentance through me.

I cannot remember everything I'm called to, but **JESUS REMEMBERS**, and Jesus is in me.

"He has remembered His covenant forever."
~ Psalm 105:8

Jesus remembered the promise of His covenant, establishing it forever through the shedding of His blood. He now calls us to partake of this covenant meal, "in remembrance of Him." But it's really a meal that celebrates how *He* remembered *us*. Jesus remembers. And Jesus is in me. Therefore, Jesus can remember through me.

I cannot persevere like I'm called to, but **JESUS PERSEVERED**, and Jesus is in me.

"For the joy set before Him Jesus endured the cross, scorning its shame, and sat down at the right hand of the throne of God."
~ Hebrews 12:2

Jesus' entire life was marked by perseverance. He endured the religious leaders who tried to trap him. He endured his disciples who never seemed to "get it." He endured betrayal, denial and desertion. He endured the physical pain of flogging and crucifixion. He endured all the way to the finish line of redemption, where He literally cried out, "It is finished!" Jesus persevered. And Jesus is in me. Therefore, Jesus can persevere through me.

I cannot live out the humility I'm called to, but
JESUS IS HUMBLE, and Jesus is in me.

> "I tell you the truth, the Son can do nothing by Himself; He can do only what He sees His Father doing... By Myself I can do nothing."
> ~ John 5:19, 30

Jesus is the Second Person of the Trinity, who spoke the universe into existence (John 1), and now holds it together (Col 1). If there was ever someone who could live a life of self-sufficiency, it is Jesus. But Jesus lived in constant dependence upon His Father for everything He did. Jesus is humble. And Jesus is in me. Therefore, Jesus can live out His humility through me.

Jesus in Me > Me Trying to Be

'Jesus in me' means when I fall short of what God's Word calls me to (which will happen), I don't have to despair. I can rest in the truth that God sees Jesus when He looks at me. I still need to repent when I mess up, but not out of fear, thinking I had better get it right or else await God's wrath. No, I can repent now with *thanksgiving*, knowing Jesus has already done *for* me everything God is looking for *from* me. And rather than that moving me to complacency, it compels me to love Jesus and live for Jesus – such that I begin to look more like Jesus.

That's the path to true transformation.

That's what begins to happen when the veil of Heaven is pulled back and we see Jesus and all that He's done for us: transformation. That's what we need more than anything else. Not another sermon, telling us what to do for *Him*. But an unveiling of what He did for *us*. And when the spiritual eyes of our hearts are opened to that, we'll be so overcome by the gospel that we'll *want* to hear what He has to say to us. And then when He does speak to us (as He does in these Seven Letters) – we'll *want* to listen, so that He can do in us and through us whatever He wants to do.

Imagine what our lives would be like if we allowed Jesus to live out these seven words in and through us. Imagine what our churches would be like. Imagine what our world would be like.

We would be transformed.
Our churches would be transformed.
The world would be transformed.

It starts with a revelation of Jesus.

> "I keep asking that the God of our Lord Jesus Christ, the glorious Father, may give you the Spirit of wisdom and revelation, so that you may know him better. I pray that the eyes of your heart may be enlightened in order that you may know the hope to which he has called you, the riches of his glorious inheritance in his holy people, and his incomparably great power for us who believe."
> ~ Ephesians 1:17-19

END NOTES

1. Edgar C. Whisenant, *88 Reasons Why the Rapture Will Be in 1988* (Whisenant/World Bible Society, 1988).

2. Edgar C. Whisenant, *The Final Shout Rapture Report 1989* (Whisenant/World Bible Society, 1989).

3. G.K. Chesterton, *Orthodoxy* (New York, NY: Doubleday Dell Publishing Group, 1990) p. 17.

4. Darrell Johnson, *Discipleship on the Edge* (Vancouver, BC: Regent College Publishing, 2004), p.14

5. Ibid, p. 51

6. https://lifehopeandtruth.com/prophecy/revelation/seven-churches-of-revelation/ (Artwork by Kelly Cunningham)

7. Johnson, *Discipleship on the Edge*, p. 40.

8. David Prior, *Message of 1 Corinthians: Life in the Local Church* (Downers Grove, IL: Intervarsity Press, 1985), p. 51.

9. Johnson, *Discipleship on the Edge*, pp. 55-56.

10. Paraphrase of J.I. Packer, *Knowing God* (Downers Grove, IL: Intervarsity Press, 1973), pp. 25-26.

11. John Ortberg, *Everybody's Normal Till You Get to Know Them* (Grand Rapids, Mich: Zondervan, 2003), p. 33.

12. Gottfried Osei-Mensah, *God's Message to the Churches* (Achimota, Ghana: Africa Christian Press, 1985), p. 20.

13. Paraphrase of Matthew 16:24-25.

14. Paraphrase of John Ortberg, *If You Want to Walk on Water, You've Got to Get Out of the Boat* (Grand Rapids, Mich: Zondervan, 2001), p. 53.

15. Oswald Chambers, *My Utmost for His Highest* (Grand Rapids, Mich: Discovery House Publishers, 1963), August 18 entry.

16. Nik Ripken, *The Insanity of God* (Nashville, TN: B&H Publishing Group, 2013), pp. 262-63.

17. Erwin McManus, *The Barbarian Way* (Nashville, TN: Thomas Nelson, 2005), p. 48.

18. Paraphrase from Ortberg, *If You Want to Walk on Water, You've Got to Get Out of the Boat,* p. 123.

19. Erwin McManus, *Chasing Daylight* (Nashville, TN: Thomas Nelson, 2002), p. 101

20. Johnson, *Discipleship on the Edge*, p. 79.

21. Randy Alcorn, *The Purity Principle* (Sisters, OR: Multnomah Publishers, 2003), p. 42.

22. Ibid., pp. 45-46.

23. Johnson, *Discipleship on the Edge*, p. 89.

24. Leslie Griffiths, "Haiti Makes Voodoo Official," April 30, 2003, http://news.bbc.co.uk/2/hi/americas/2985627.stm.

25. Robert Mounce, "The Book of Revelation," in *The New International Commentary on the New Testament* (Grand Rapids, Mich: Eerdmans Publishing Co., 1977), p. 104.

26. Craig Keener, "The Book of Revelation," in The NIV Application Commentary (Grand Rapids, Mich: Zondervan, 2000), p. 139.

27. Ibid.

28. Rosaria Butterfield, "Love Your Neighbor Enough to Speak Truth," October 31, 2016, https://www.thegospelcoalition.org/article/love-your-neighbor-enough-to-speak-truth/.

29. Randy Alcorn, *The Truth and Grace Paradox* (Sisters, OR: Multnomah Publishers, 2003), p.17.

END NOTES

30. Bonhoeffer, *Life Together* (New York, NY: Harper Row, 1954), pp. 110-111.

31. Kyle Ideman, *Not a Fan* (Grand Rapids, Mich: Zondervan, 2011), pp. 13-14.

32. Paraphrase of Idleman, *Not a Fan*, p. 59.

33. J.M. Hirsch, Associated Press, "Meet the Flexitarians," March 16, 2004, https://www.cbsnews.com/news/meet-the-flexitarians/.

34. Idleman, *Not a Fan*, p. 202

35. John Eldredge, *The Journey of Desire* (Nashville, TN: Thomas Nelson, 2000), p. 199.

36. Samuel Johnson: Quoted in C.S. Lewis, *Mere Christianity* (New York, NY: MacMillan Publishing, 1960), p. 78.

37. Darrell Johnson, *Discipleship on the Edge*, p. 98.

38. NASA, "Muscle Atrophy", http://www.nasa.gov/pdf/64249main_ffs_factsheets_hbp_atrophy.pdf

39. John Ortberg, *If You Want to Walk on Water, You've got to Get out of the Boat*, p. 47.

40. John MacArthur, "Revelation 1-11," in The MacArthur New Testament Commentary (Chicago, IL: Moody, 1999), p. 109.

41. Sister Connection is a holistic ministry that serves widows and orphans in Burundi. www.sisterconnection.org.

42. Paraphrase of David Platt, *Follow Me* (Carol Stream, IL: Tyndale House, 2013), p. 216.

43. Gottfried Osei-Mensah, *God's Message to the Churches*, p. 61.

44. Ibid., p. 61.

45. Ibid., pp. 56-57.

46. Erwin McManus, *Chasing Daylight*, pp. 41-42.

47. Gottfried Osei-Mensah, *God's Message to the Churches*, p. 58.

48. David Prior, *Message of 1 Corinthians: Life in the Local Church*, p. 51.

49. Terry Fisher, San Mateo, California. Quoted in *Preaching Resources*, Spring 1996, p. 69.

50. John Ortberg, *When the Game is Over It All Goes Back in the Box* (Grand Rapids, Mich: Zondervan, 2007), pp. 78-79.

51. Priya Joshi, International Business Times, "Iraq: Four Youths Beheaded By Isis for Refusing to Renounce Christian Faith," December 13, 2014, http://www.ibtimes.co.uk/iraq-four-youths-beheaded-by-isis-refusing-renounce-christian-faith-1479339

52. Craig Keener, "The Book of Revelation" in the NIV Application Commentary, p. 154.

53. Randy Alcorn, *Heaven* (Wheaton, IL: Tyndale House, 2004), xxii.

54. Darrell Johnson, *Discipleship on the Edge*, p. 122.

55. Ibid.

56. Ibid.

57. John Ortberg, *When the Game is Over It All Goes Back in the Box*, pp. 119-120.

58. C.S. Lewis, *Mere Christianity* (New York, NY: Touchstone, 1996), pp. 175-176.

Lightning Source UK Ltd.
Milton Keynes UK
UKHW021545230719
346677UK00007B/1113/P